POEMS 1955–1959

and

AN ESSAY IN AUTOBIOGRAPHY

BORIS LEONIDOVICH PASTERNAK was born in Moscow in 1890. His father was an artist and his mother was a concert pianist, and the family numbered Tolstoy, Scriabin and Rilke among their friends. He received a classical education and, under Scriabin's influence, began to study music intensively. In 1912, he abandoned music and went to Marburg to study philosophy, but a year later he was back in Moscow having decided to give up philosophy and devote himself entirely to poetry. His first two ebullient collections, *A Twin in the Clouds* and *Above the Barriers* appeared in 1912 and 1917 respectively. But it was not until 1922, with the appearance of *My Sister, Life* – his poetic response to the hopeful revolutionary summer of 1917 – that he triumphantly achieved his own distinctive voice. He was married in 1921, and again in 1934, and lived most of his life in Moscow. In the Twenties and Thirties he began writing fiction, including *The Childhood of Luvers* (1922) and *The Last Summer* (1934), as well as attempting a more "epic" poetry in an effort to stay in touch with the literary requirements of the new régime. The results included *Nineteen Five, Lieutenant Schmidt* (both 1927), and *Spektorsky* (1931), a "novel in verse". At about this time, he began translating European literature into Russian. As his life became increasingly difficult this was to become his main source of income; his translations of Shakespeare and Goethe are generally regarded as masterpieces of the translator's art. In 1932, *Second Birth* – a book of poems which celebrated his love for the woman who was to become his second wife – appeared to mark a new beginning. However, it was not until the early-Forties that the longed for new beginning truly came about. The clear, restrained, but still evocative style of *On Early Trains* (1943) would serve him well for his last works: the poems in the present collection, *An Essay in Autobiography* (1957) and his masterpiece, *Doctor Zhivago*. With the publication of *Doctor Zhivago* in the West in 1957–8 and with his acceptance of the Nobel Prize for Literature in 1958, official pressure intensified. After an unprecedented and savage campaign of denunciation, he was forced to renounce the award. He died on 30 May 1960.

By Boris Pasternak and
available in Harvill editions

DOCTOR ZHIVAGO

About Boris Pasternak and
available in Harvill editions ·

BORIS PASTERNAK: THE TRAGIC YEARS 1930–60
by his son Evgeny Pasternak

Boris Pasternak

POEMS 1955–1959

Translated from the Russian by
Michael Harari

AN ESSAY IN AUTOBIOGRAPHY

Translated from the Russian by
Manya Harari

WITH AN INTRODUCTION BY CRAIG RAINE

HEREFORD AND WORCESTER
COUNTY LIBRARIES
90   104190

891
.714

COLLINS HARVILL
8 Grafton Street, London W1
1990

COLLINS HARVILL
William Collins Sons and Co Ltd
London · Glasgow · Sydney · Auckland
Toronto · Johannesburg

BRITISH LIBRARY CATALOGUING IN PUBLICATION DATA
Pasternak, Boris *1890–1960*
Poems 1955–1959; and an essay in autobiography.
1. Fiction in Russian. Pasternak, Boris, 1890–1960–
Biographies
I. Title II. Pasternak, Boris *1890–1960*.
891.71'42

ISBN 0–00–271065–x

An Essay in Autobiography first published in Great Britain
by Collins and Harvill Press 1959
Poems 1955–1959 first published in Great Britain
by Collins and Harvill Press 1960
This joint paperback edition first published by Collins Harvill 1990

Poems in Part One © Giangiacomo Feltrinelli Editore, Milan, 1959
Poems in Part Two © William Collins Sons and Co Ltd, London, 1960
Translation of *Poems 1955–1959* © William Collins Sons and Co Ltd 1960
An Essay in Autobiography © Giangiacomo Feltrinelli Editore, Milan, 1959
This revised translation of *An Essay in Autobiography*
© William Collins Sons and Co Ltd 1959, 1990
Introduction © Craig Raine 1990

All rights reserved. This book is sold subject to the condition that it
shall not, by way of trade or otherwise, be lent, re-sold, hired out or
otherwise circulated without the publisher's prior consent in any
form of binding or cover other than that in which it is published and
without a similar condition including this condition being imposed
upon the subsequent purchaser.

Printed and bound in Great Britain by
Hartnolls Limited, Bodmin, Cornwall

CONTENTS

INTRODUCTION

Titles mattered to Pasternak. He came to regret as pretentious the title he gave his first volume of poetry, *A Twin in the Clouds*. He always wanted to change Scriabin's *L'Extase* to something less reminiscent of "a tight soap wrapper".

Like Lenin, who was born Vladimir Ilyich Ulyanov, Pasternak's *An Essay in Autobiography* started life innocuously enough under a different name. At the instigation of Nikolay Bannikov, his editor at Goslitizdat, Pasternak completed these memoirs in May and June of 1956. At that stage, they were entitled "Instead of a Foreword" and intended to introduce a one volume edition of his poetry. By November 1957, Pasternak had corrected the proofs. On 22 November, *Il Dottor Živago* was published in Italy and launched at the Hotel Intercontinental in Milan by the publisher Giangiacomo Feltrinelli. From that moment on, Pasternak's memoir was no longer innocuous. When it eventually appeared in the Soviet Union in January 1967, it was slightly abridged for *Novy Mir* and under yet another alias – like the dangerous character it had become – *People and Circumstances*. In the interval, it had been published worldwide – in America as *I Remember – A Sketch in Autobiography*. Only in Italy, where it was entitled *Autobiografia e nuovi versi*, did the book fulfil Pasternak's original conception – of a volume consisting of newly composed poems and poems which had previously appeared only in periodicals.* However, at some stage, Goslitizdat's offer was for, as Guy de Mallac puts it, "a large volume of Pasternak's poetry (including all the Zhivago poems except 'Hamlet')". Even earlier, Pasternak himself may have intended the essay to introduce his collected works, including *Doctor Zhivago*. At any rate, this joint volume of prose and poetry goes some way towards meeting Pasternak's intention of thirty years ago.

Just as *An Essay in Autobiography* has several *noms de guerre*, so it isn't Pasternak's only attempt at the genre. It has a cloudy twin, the memoir *Safe Conduct*, which Pasternak began in the late Twenties and which was published, before appearing in book form, in separate parts from 1929 to 1931 in the journals *Zvezda* and *Krasnaya nov*. Though *Safe Conduct* covers the same period of time and some of the same topics, *An Essay in Autobiography* successfully avoids repetition, is much more readable and quite self-standing. Its approaches are different; it adds a lot of welcome and necessary self-irony; it excises a great many passages of inspissated aesthetic speculation, and brings the story, if not up to date, at least to the point where it can briefly bring back to life Marina Tsvetayeva and Pasternak's Georgian friends, Paolo Yashvili and Titsian Tabidze, all

* See *Boris Pasternak: The Tragic Years 1930–60* by Evgeny Pasternak, Collins Harvill, London, 1990.

vii

three of whom, in their various ways, were victims of Stalin's terror. Pasternak sets down the history of his acquaintance with Tsvetayeva and his feelings of guilt and inadequacy quite frankly, courting neither punishment nor exoneration, in a testimony to the complication of truth that is moving because matter of fact – in the deepest as well as the most obvious sense. We see the Georgian friends toasting Pasternak's black eye at an hilarious, tipsy supper. The nearest Pasternak approaches to the time of composition is in a brief, compassionate reference to the suicide of Alexander Fadeyev in 1956 – an allusion justified by Pasternak's analysis of Mayakovsky's suicide.

But that black eye is important because it illustrates a crucial difference between *Safe Conduct* and *An Essay in Autobiography*. This is Pasternak's increasing indifference to conventional ideas of dignity and a tardy but acute sense of the ridiculous, particularly as applied to himself. In *Safe Conduct*, the young Pasternak is convinced of the importance of being earnest, and the self-importance, too – a common enough tendency in young artists, as Joyce memorably recorded in *Ulysses* where the young Stephen earnestly bows to himself in the mirror. *Safe Conduct* recalls the visit to Marburg of two sisters, one of whom Boris loved. Seeing off the pair at Marburg station, the young man, convinced his farewells had been inadequate, sprinted down the platform with the departing train and finally clung to it, so that, tear-stained and emotional, he had to be hauled on board by the guard. In cheap lodgings at Berlin, the young Pasternak sits by a table through the night, maintaining a particular posture: "I have described the position of my body with such accuracy," he writes, without a flicker of amusement, "because this had also been its position that morning on the step of the moving train and it had memorised the posture. It was the position of someone fallen from a lofty eminence which had long sustained and carried him but had then let him fall and rushed on noisily over his head, vanishing forever round a turning."

There is less of this risibly lofty guff in *An Essay in Autobiography*, where, instead, Pasternak wryly observes himself as a young boy, at a time when he imagined he had once been a girl – "and that I could regain this earlier more pleasing, more fascinating personality, by pulling in my belt so tight I almost fainted." In his *Confessions*, Rousseau, that great dealer in the endearingly discreditable, offers his reader a contradictory analysis of his narrative indiscretions. On the one hand, their purpose is to demonstrate the uniqueness of Rousseau, to vindicate his claim that he is "not made like any of those who are in existence" because, after producing him in an edition of one, Nature broke the mould. On the other hand, Rousseau argues, only a paragraph later, for the concept of human identity and solidarity: will anyone read these memoirs honestly, he asks, and retort, "I was better than that man". We all recognise the belt-tightening fantasy element in childhood and cannot say we are "better than that man". In *Safe Conduct*, Pasternak is rather too keen on savouring the flavour of his own uniqueness – his sensitivity, his passion, the meniscus of his emotions. *An Essay in Autobiography*, however, is much more aware of human solidarity and silliness.

Pasternak tells us there that he spoke with "a fake *Berliner* accent" – a piece of absurd vanity which had a humiliating sequel told only by his brother, Alexander, in his memoirs, *A Vanished Present*.* The essay also deplores the "stupid pretentiousness" of calling his first book *A Twin in the Clouds*, a piece of foolishness cognate with the fashionable behaviour of his youth when "the proper thing was to be insolent and strut about sticking one's nose in the air". But Pasternak reserves his harshest judgement not for this foolishness, but for his own weak malleability: "although it sickened me, I tagged along not to be left behind." He allowed Bobrov to inaugurate and conduct quarrels for him, though his own instincts were pacific. He let himself be talked into writing Gorky "an idiotic letter, full of ignorance, conceit and affectation". Pasternak is not out to show himself in a good light.

It is hardly surprising, therefore, that the older, self-critical Pasternak should dismiss his earlier attempt, *Safe Conduct*, as a book "spoiled by its affected manner, the besetting sin of those days". More generally, he pronounces damningly on his early output: "I dislike my style before 1940, just as I quarrel with half of Mayakovsky's writings and with some of Yesenin's. I dislike the disintegrating forms, the impoverished thought and the littered and uneven language of those days."

Broadly, Pasternak is right. It would be easy to quote from *Safe Conduct* long passages where the "thought" is little more than syntax in a state of fuddled exaltation. And yet *Safe Conduct* cannot be disowned in the brisk manner Pasternak proposes. It is recognisably the work of the same man who wrote *An Essay in Autobiography* – recognisable in its strengths and its weaknesses, which continue, however modified, into the later work. *Safe Conduct* isn't utterly devoid either of self-irony or self-criticism, though the early work can't match the cool urbanity of the later, whose detachment appears to be modelled on Scriabin's "wordly manner of putting on a superficial air and avoiding serious subjects". Not that Pasternak is ever frivolous; only that, in *An Essay in Autobiography*, he is less clenched and frowning, more relaxed and smiling.

The differences exist, then, but so do the similarities. The fake *Berliner* accent isn't so very different, after all, from *Safe Conduct*'s bogus Italian dialect "made up from earlier attempts to read Dante in the original". There are, too, moments of characteristically unforgiving self-criticism in *Safe Conduct*: on first meeting Mayakovsky, the young Pasternak feels "totally bereft of talent" and later on dismisses a quarrel with Mayakovsky as "a piece of senseless affectation on my part". *Affectation* – the very word so favoured by the older writer.

An Essay in Autobiography has moments of vivid brilliance, yet all of them can be matched by quotations from the rich and wayward pages of *Safe Conduct*. The human observation is of a piece: in the *Essay*, we see and

* *A Vanished Present* by Alexander Pasternak, Oxford, 1984.

hear the Trubetskoys at the University lecturing "in imploring accents and in droning, whining voices with an aristocratic lisp"; in *Safe Conduct*, the philosopher Samarin "arming himself with a dry biscuit, used it like a choirmaster's tuning fork to beat out the logical divisions of his argument". Pasternak's laconic, unpoetic poetry is also of a piece: in the *Essay*, Venice is portrayed "swelling like a biscuit soaked in tea", while *Safe Conduct* shows us slush like "icy kvass-soaked bread" and gives us a Venice whose side canals are dark as offal, "full of dead rats and dancing melon peel", above which the Milky Way is like a shedding dandelion. In the *Essay*, there is the brilliant metaphoric trope which assimilates old men's grey bald spots to smoke rings; in *Safe Conduct*, the younger writer notices, with equal brilliance, that the smoke from a cigar is like a tortoise-shell comb.

In fact, *An Essay in Autobiography* is economical with its writerly gifts, where *Safe Conduct* is clumsy but prodigal. The later work can give us "grubby" snowflakes like dropped stitches – a simile at once lucid and just and original – but *Safe Conduct*, for all its faults, is the richer in purely literary terms. A list: "the heavy capstan of the seasons", a "reeking gallery" of empty wicker flower hampers "with sonorous Italian frankmarks", the leather bellows at the joints of a long train of coaches, stations "like moths made of stone, they rushed by and fled to the rear of the train", Mayakovsky straddling a chair like a motorbike, talking, and leaving behind "half-eaten cakes and glasses blinded with hot milk". The gift in *Safe Conduct* is extraordinary – padded cadets learning to fence "pecked at one another like cockerels in sacks" – and so is the pretentiousness.

By the time of *An Essay in Autobiography*, Pasternak had both more or less under control. There he describes a journey by sleigh with Zbarsky which is tour de force of accurate observation, in which there are no intricate metaphors to dazzle or distract. Pasternak is less interested in brilliance, more interested in overall success. But a key passage in the *Essay* concerns the death of Tolstoy because it shows clearly how Pasternak has achieved control over his gifts and his susceptibilities. Almost at once, Pasternak yields to temptation: "Tolstoy's presence filled the room like a mountain – say like Elbrus – or like a storm cloud the size of half a sky." This is recognisably the febrile mode of the worst of *Safe Conduct* and the worst of the letters exchanged between Rilke, Pasternak and Tsvetayeva. It is followed by an opaque digression about Pushkin and then, just as one fears the worst, Pasternak revokes, in a section of wry, minutely observed realism, everything which has gone before: "but what there was in the far corner of the room was not a mountain but a wrinkled little old man, one of the dozens of old men invented by Tolstoy and scattered through his books." And Pasternak drops the evocative to concentrate on the actual – the fir saplings around the bed, the sheaves of light, the shadow of the cross thrown by the window, the local restaurant's brisk trade in "underdone" beef steaks served to the world's press.

Yet just as we applaud the way in which the dry has overtaken the splashy mode, Pasternak indulges two characteristic weaknesses – the "poetic" flouting of reality and the glib encapsulation. Both run counter to his gift for the anti-poetic – a gift which he admired in Mayakovsky and which he possessed in abundance himself, though he modestly pretended to amazement when he identified it in the other's poetry: "I had never heard anything like it before. Everything was there in it: the boulevards, the dogs, the poplars and the butterflies, the barbers, bakers, tailors and locomotives." The mundane was always a resource for Pasternak, as we can illustrate from *Safe Conduct* when he compares the endlessly reiterated goodbyes to Scriabin to "a collar stud that simply refused to slip into its narrow aperture". Nothing could be farther from this gift than the more operatic brand of poetry which tends to turn on some wonky impossibility, as if the impossibility itself were the guarantee of afflatus. In the Tolstoy passage, Pasternak concludes with a cloying poetic fiction in which the heroes and heroines created by Tolstoy unknowingly pass in the train the little station of Astapovo where his body lies dead. For a finale, Pasternak gives in to his weakness for epitome: "as we might speak of the passionate quality of Lermentov, of Tyutchev's fecundity of thought, of Chekhov's poetry, of Gogol's …" It is difficult to take this high-flown Parnassian seriously. The verdicts are served up like *petit fours* in a cloud of hieratic incense. There isn't much of this in *An Essay in Autobiography* but there is enough of it to show that the author of *Safe Conduct* and the author of the later work are closely related – perhaps even the same gifted, brilliant, simple, down-to-earth person who could be tempted by the noise of sounding generalisations.

The other half of this book is the poetry, about which I am even less qualified to speak than about the prose. I have recently translated several hundred lines of Pasternak's poetry with my wife, Ann Pasternak Slater, who speaks Russian.* The experience encourages me to comment, if timidly, about translation. We translate because, although, according to Robert Frost, poetry is what is lost in translation, we have D. J. Enright's word for it that even more is lost if poetry isn't translated. Pasternak himself was a translator and *An Essay in Autobiography* includes two asides about translation which are germane and not particularly encouraging. About Rilke, he says, "In Russia Rilke is unknown. The few translations of him have been unsuccessful. The translators are not to blame. They are used to conveying meaning but not tone, and in Rilke tone is everything." And of Georgy Leonidze, he says, he is "the most independent of all poets, the one closest to the secrets of his language and therefore least translatable". Pasternak is just such a poet – a poet from whom we learn that translation is necessary and impossible. Pasternak's sound effects are of paramount importance and virtually unreproduceable in English, or in any other language but Russian I would imagine. Take the poem "In Hospital". The first line of the third stanza is a list of what the dying person sees from the ambulance window– *militsia, ulitsa, litsa*.

* See *Boris Pasternak: The Tragic Years 1930–60*.

In English, this thickly-woven sound pattern is utterly lost: *policemen, streets, faces*. Any attempt to reproduce it and be faithful to the sense is futile. Pasternak's brief lists are one of the glories of his poetry: in the same poem, stanza six, one encounters *k palatam, polam, i khalatam*, a densely assonantal line which is untranslatable except weakly as "wards, floors, doctor's gowns".

Another difficulty with Pasternak is his tendency, like Emily Dickinson, to tell the truth "but tell it slant". In one's own language, one can rely on the reader to see the slant and make the correction. In another language, though, the slant can't be reproduced without fatally adding to the confusion: the translator must translate the corrected, adjusted version to some degree, or risk losing the reader entirely. A further difficulty facing the translator is how far to succumb to the foreign idiom of the original. My own preference is to resist absolutely and aim for a poem which is at least English. Yet I can appreciate that readers develop a tolerance for foreign flavours in their translations as a spurious guarantee of authenticity. The "flaw" actually has a positive effect on the reader. Christopher Logue's marvellous versions of Homer in *War Music* are at once boldly vernacular and yet faintly archaic and more Latinate than is normally permissible in English poetry proper – in a way that affects us as a real taste of Homer.

My mother-in-law's translations of her brother's poetry have their flaws as English poetry, yet they reproduce like no other translations some of the rhythmic complexities of Pasternak's work, and I wasn't at all surprised when Seamus Heaney and the American poet, Tom Sleigh, confessed rather shyly to me in Harvard that they found the versions of Lydia Pasternak Slater, in a curious way, the most authentic versions of Pasternak. In spite of their un-Englishness, I wanted to add at the time. Now, I suspect it was because of their un-Englishness.

The translations here are by Michael Harari and are to be welcomed once again as a brave attempt at the impossible. Having translated some of these poems myself, I am in a position to appreciate his skill and his tenacity and resourcefulness. It isn't enough, of course, but it is the best we can do.

CRAIG RAINE
Oxford
July, 1989

AN ESSAY IN
AUTOBIOGRAPHY

1 . EARLY CHILDHOOD

In *Safe Conduct*, an experiment in autobiography, written in the Twenties, I described the circumstances which have shaped my life. Unfortunately, the book was spoiled by its affected manner, the besetting sin of those days.

I can't avoid retelling some of the events in the present sketch, but I will do my best not to repeat myself.

I was born in 1890 in Moscow, on 29 January according to the Old Calendar,[1] in Lyzhin's house opposite the Seminary in Oruzheiny Street. Surprisingly, something has remained in my memory of my walks in autumn with my wet-nurse[2] in the Seminary park – sodden paths heaped with fallen leaves, ponds and artificial hills, the painted Seminary turnpikes, the noisy games and fights of the seminarists during their recreation.

Facing the gates of the Seminary there was a two-storeyed stone house; it had a courtyard for the cabbies, and our flat was above the vaulted archway of the courtyard entrance.

My impressions of my early childhood are made up of the elements of terror and ecstasy. They ascend in fairytale colours towards two central images which ruled my world and gave it unity: one is of the stuffed bears in the coach-makers' windows in Coachmakers Row; the other is of a kindly, shaggy, stooping giant with a deep gruff voice (this was the publisher Konchalovsky), and it includes his family, and their flat, and the pictures on its walls – sketches in pencil, wash and pen-and-ink, by Serov, Vrubel, my father and the brothers Vasnetsov.

Our neighbourhood was extremely sordid; it was close to the Tverskiye-Yamskiye, the Pipe and the lanes of the Tsvetnoy.[3] You were always being dragged away; you were not supposed to hear this, you were not allowed to know that. But sometimes nannies and wet-nurses wearied of isolation, and then we were surrounded by all sorts of company.

And at noon the mounted police drilled on the parade ground of the Znamensky Barracks.

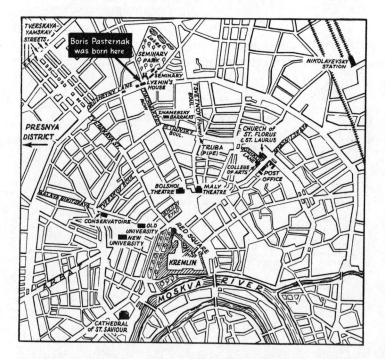

As a result of all this rubbing shoulders with beggars and women-pilgrims, and of nearness to the world of the rejected and of listening to their stories of troubles and hysterics, I was filled too early and for life with a compassion for women, so terrible that it was hardly to be borne, and with a still more anguished pity for my parents who would die before me and whom it was my duty to deliver from the pains of hell by some shining deed, unheard-of and unique.

When I was three we moved to official quarters at the College of Arts.[4] This was in Myasnitskaya,[5] opposite the main Post Office. Our flat was in an annexe across the yard, separate from the main building.

The building was old, beautiful and remarkable in many ways. The fire of 1812[6] had spared it. In the previous century, under the Empress Catherine, it had been the secret refuge of a Masonic Lodge. One corner, at the intersection of Myasnitskaya and Yushkov Lane, had a pillared, semi-circular balcony; part of it formed a recess and communicated with the College hall. From it, you could have a clear view of the Myasnitskaya running into the distance towards the railway stations.

From this balcony the inhabitants of the building watched the ceremony of transferring the remains of the Emperor Alexander III in 1894 and two years later saw part of the festivities in honour of the coronation of Nicholas II.

Standing near the balustrade, among a crowd of students and professors, my mother held me up in her arms. An abyss opened at her feet. At the bottom of it was the empty roadway strewn with sand. The street waited, holding its breath. Officers bustled about, shouting orders in loud voices, but they were inaudible to the onlookers on the balcony, as if the stillness of the breathless thousands whom the soldiers kept pushing from the roadway back on to the edges of the kerb had swallowed up the sounds, like sand swallowing water. Slowly, mournfully, the bells rang out. A wave gathered out of the distance and rolled past into the distance beyond, stirring a sea of hands as Moscow bared its head and crossed itself. To the sound of bells tolling on every side, the procession advanced endlessly – troops, clergy, horses plumed and draped in black, a catafalque of inconceivable magnificence and heralds in the curious costumes of a bygone age. On they went, past houses muffled and upholstered in black; the funeral flags hung downcast.

The spirit of pomp and ceremony was inseparable from the College which was under the ægis of the Ministry of the Imperial Court. The Grand Duke Sergey Alexandrovich was its patron and he came regularly to its exhibitions and its speech days. The Grand Duke was thin and lanky. Shielding their sketch-books with their hats, Serov and my father drew caricatures of him at the receptions which he attended at the Golitsins' and Yakunchikovs'.

Facing the wicket-gate of a small garden shaded by ancient trees, the annexe where we lived rose above the sheds and offices in the yard. Hot lunches were served to students in the basement, and an everlasting smell of fried cutlets and pasties cooked in batter hung over the stairs. Our flat was on the first landing. The College Clerk lived on the floor above.

Half a century later, I read the following under the heading "1894" on page 125 of a recent Soviet book, *Moscow in the Life and Work of Leo Tolstoy* by N. S. Rodionov:

> On 23 November, Tolstoy and his daughters went to a concert given at the flat of the painter Leonid Pasternak, Director of the College of Arts. The musicians were Pasternak's wife, the 'cellist Brandukov and the violinist Grzhimaldi, both Professors at the Conservatoire.

This is true except for one small error. The Director of the College was not my father but Prince Lvov.

I remember that evening perfectly. I had been put to bed, but late in the night I was aroused by such a sweet, nostalgic torment as I had not experienced in the same degree before. I cried out and wept in fear and anguish. But the music drowned my cries and it was not until the end of the movement that anyone heard me. Then the curtain which hung across the room, dividing it in two, was pushed aside. My mother came in, bent over me and soon calmed me down. She may have carried me into the drawing-room, or perhaps I only saw it through the open door. The air was filled with tobacco smoke; the candles blinked as if it stung their eyes. They shone on the red varnished wood of the 'cello and of the violin. The piano loomed black. The men were in black frock-coats. Women leaned out of their shoulder-high dresses like flowers out of flower baskets. Like smoke rings, the grey-ringed heads of two or three old men drifted together. One of them was the painter Gué, whom I was later to know well and see often. The image of another has been present to me, as to most people, all my life: to me especially because my father illustrated his work, went to see him, honoured him, and indeed our whole house was permeated by his spirit. This was Lev Nikolayevich[7]. . . .

Why then did I cry so bitterly and why do I remember my anxiety so well? I was used to the sound of the piano – my mother was an accomplished pianist; to me it was inseparable from that of music itself. But the voices of strings – particularly strings combined in chamber music – were unfamiliar and as disturbing as if they had been real voices carried through the open window from the street, calling for help and announcing a disaster.

It was, I think, the winter of two deaths – Anton Rubinstein's and Tchaikovsky's.[8] The music was probably Tchaikovsky's famous "Trio".

That evening marked for me the end of my unconscious early childhood. From then on, my memory functioned and my consciousness was active and unbroken by long gaps, as in an adult.

Every spring the Travelling Exhibition[9] was held in the College show rooms. The pictures arrived from Petersburg in the winter and were stored in sheds – there was a row of them outside our back windows. A little before Easter the crates were brought out into the yard. The College servants prised them open and unscrewed the heavy picture frames from the boards; then each picture was carried by two men across the yard to the main building. Perched on the window-sills we watched excitedly. That was how we first saw many pictures by Russian masters,[10] which to-day are famous and make up half the contents of the public galleries and State collections.

It was only at the beginning that the group of painters[11] with whom my father was connected took part in these shows. Later they founded their own younger associations, "The Union of Russian Artists".[12]

In the late Nineties the sculptor Pavel Trubetskoy, who had spent his life in Italy, arrived in Moscow. A studio with a glass roof was built on to the back of our house and put at his disposal. Our kitchen window which used to look out on the yard now looked into his workroom. Through it we could watch him and his caster, Robecchi, at work, and see his models – not only children and ballerinas, but mounted Cossacks and even carriages and pairs which drove easily into the lofty studio through its wide gateway.

It was also from our kitchen that my father's remarkable illustrations to Tolstoy's *Resurrection* were dispatched.

The novel appeared, chapter by chapter in *Niva*,[13] a periodical edited by the Petersburg publisher Marx. It came out regularly and on time. My father worked feverishly to meet the deadline.

But Tolstoy often held up the proofs and altered them so much that the drawings made for the original version had to be changed. Luckily Father's notebooks were filled with sketches of the courtrooms, transit prisons,[14] villages and trains which formed so many of Tolstoy's backgrounds. This stock of living details and the realism which he shared with Tolstoy allowed him to keep close to the text.

To save time, the drawings were sent off by hand; the guards on the express trains to Petersburg acted as messen-gers. My imagination was impressed by the sight of a uniformed guard waiting outside our kitchen door, as on a station platform outside a railway carriage.

Joiner's glue sizzled on the range. The drawings were hastily sprinkled with fixative and glued on sheets of cardboard, and the parcels, wrapped up, tied and sealed, were handed over to the guard.

2. SCRIABIN

The second decade of my life was very different from the first. Moscow in the Nineties, in all the splendour of her "sixteen hundred belfries",[1] still had the look of a remote, provincial town as picturesque as in a fairytale, but with something of the legendary grandeur of the Third Rome[2] or of the mythic capitals of the old Russian epics. Ancient customs were still observed. In the autumn, horses were blessed in Yushkov Lane which ran between the College and the Church of St Florus and St Laurus,[3] who were regarded as patrons of horse-breeders; the horses and the grooms and coachmen who brought them crowded the church precincts and the Lane as if it were a horse fair.

It seemed to me as a child that the advent of the new century changed everything as at the stroke of a magic wand. The city was gripped by the same financial frenzy as were the leading capitals of the world. Tall blocks of offices and flats sprang up overnight in an epidemic of speculative deals. All at once, brick giants reached into the sky from every street. And with them, Moscow, outstripping Petersburg, produced a new Russian art, the art of a big city, young, fresh and contemporary.

The College was affected by the same fever as the rest of the town. Its allocation from the Treasury was not sufficient for its upkeep; so private business men were asked to raise funds to cover the budget. It was decided to build and let many-storeyed blocks of flats on the College grounds, and glass-roofed premises suitable for exhibitions on the site of the garden. At the end of the Nineties the sheds and out-buildings were pulled down, the garden was uprooted and deep trenches were dug in the ground. The trenches filled with water and in them, as in a pond, dead rats floated and frogs jumped and dived in off the banks. Our annexe was also scheduled for demolition.

That winter, two or three classrooms and lecture halls in the main building were converted into a new flat for us and we moved into it in 1901. As one of the apartments from which it had been carved out was round and another still more fancifully shaped, our dwelling for the next ten years had a bathroom and a box-room which together formed a crescent; the kitchen was oval and the dining-room had a semi-circle bitten out of it. There was always a muffled din coming from the passages and workrooms outside, and from the end room Professor Chaplin could be heard lecturing on heating methods to the architecture class next door.

For some years, while we were still in our old flat, I had been having lessons in preparation for going to school. Sometimes my mother taught me, sometimes private teachers were engaged. For a while, when there was a plan to send me to the Peter and Paul High School,[4] I studied at home and in German all the subjects taught in its junior form.

Of the various teachers whom I gratefully remember, I will mention the first, Yekaterina Ivanovna Baratynskaya, who wrote for children and translated children's stories from English. Starting from scratch, she showed me how to sit at table and hold a pen and taught me reading, writing and the beginnings of arithmetic and French. She lived in a furnished room where I was taken for my lessons. The room was dark and stacked from floor to ceiling with books. It smelled of cleanliness, austerity, boiled milk and burned coffee. Lace curtains hung over the window; outside it, grubby, creamy-greyish snowflakes dropped like stitches. They distracted my attention. Yekaterina Ivanovna spoke to me in French and I replied at random. When the lesson was over she wiped her pen on the lining of her jacket, waited for me to be fetched and bundled me off.

In 1901 I entered the Second Form of the Fifth Moscow High School; after Vannovsky's reform[5] it had added natural science and other modern subjects to its curriculum but had kept its classical slant and continued to teach Greek.

In the spring of 1903 Father rented a *dacha*[6] in the country, in Obolenskoye village, near to Maloyaroslavets on the Bryansk railway (now known as the Kiev Line). It turned out that Scriabin was our neighbour. We had not been on visiting terms with him until then.

The two houses stood at some distance from each other, beside a forest clearing on a hill. We arrived, as usually happens, early in the morning. The sun filtered into the rooms through the low branches which overhung our roof. Inside, bundles wrapped in sacking were cut open, and food, bed linen, frying-pans and pails unpacked. I escaped into the wood.

God Almighty, what that morning wood was filled with! The sunlight pierced it through and through from every side. Its moving shadows tilted its cap this way and that; and from its rising and falling branches came that always unexpected, always unfamiliar chirruping of birds which starts with loud, abrupt calls and, gradually dying down, repeats in its warm quick urgency the alternating lights and shadows of the trees running into the distance. And in exactly the same way as lights and shadows alternated and birds sang and fluttered from branch to branch, so fragments of the Third Symphony or *Divine Poem*, composed upon the piano in the neighbouring house, carried and resounded through the wood.

Lord, what music it was! Again and again the symphony tumbled into ruins like a shelled town and was built up and rose out of its rubble of destruction. Its content, insanely elaborate, filled it to overflowing and was new – as the forest was new, breathing life and freshness, clothed in spring that morning in 1903 – it wasn't 1803 remember! And just as in the forest there was not one leaf of coloured tinfoil or crinkled paper, so the symphony had no false depth in it, no solemn rhetoric, nothing to make it sound like Beethoven, or like Glinka, or like Ivan Ivanovich[7] or like Princess Maria Alex-evna[8]; instead, its tragic power triumphantly thumbed its nose at everything respectably decrepit and majestically dull, and was insanely, mischievously daring, and free, frivolous and elemental as a fallen angel.

You would expect a man who composed such music to know what kind of a person he was and, in his hours of leisure, to be as tranquil and lucent as God resting from his labours on the seventh day; and such indeed he proved to be.

He and my father would often go for walks along the Warsaw Highway which cut across the countryside not far from our house. Sometimes I accompanied them. Scriabin liked to take a run and then to go on skipping along the road like a stone skimming the water, as if at any moment he might leave the ground and glide on air. In general, he had trained himself in various kinds of sublime lightness and unburdened movement verging on flight. Among such expressions of his character were his well-bred charm and his worldly manner of putting on a superficial air and avoiding serious subjects in society. All the more astonishing were his paradoxes in the course of these country walks.

He argued with my father about good and evil and life and art, he attacked Tolstoy and preached Nietzsche's superman and amoralism. They agreed only in their conception of the essence and problems of craftsmanship, in everything else they differed.

I was twelve at the time. Half their arguments were above my head. But Scriabin conquered me by the freshness of his mind. I worshipped him. I was always on his side though I hardly ever knew what he meant. Soon he left for Switzerland where he was to stay for six years.[9]

That autumn I had an accident which kept us in the

country later than usual. Father was painting a picture, "To Night Pastures".[10] It was a sunset scene of girls from a nearby village, Bocharovo, riding at full tilt and driving horses to the water meadows at the bottom of our hill. One evening I joined them, but my horse ran away with me and, as it jumped a wide stream, I fell off and broke my leg. I was left with one leg shorter than the other and, as a result, was afterwards exempted from the army whenever there was a call-up.

Even before that summer I had strummed a little on the piano and had managed to put a few notes together of my own. Now, after my meeting with Scriabin, I longed passionately to compose. That autumn I began to study the theory of composition and devoted to it all my six remaining years at school; I worked with the admirable Engel, a musical critic and theoretician of that time, and later with Professor Glier.

No one had the slightest doubt of my vocation. My future was settled. My parents were delighted with my choice of a career; music was to be my destiny – and every sort of ungrateful beastliness towards my elders, whose shoes I was unworthy to unlace, every form of mulish disobedience, neglect and eccentricity were forgiven me for its sake. Even when I was caught fiddling with some problem in fugue or counterpoint at school, a music book open on my desk in the middle of a lesson in mathematics or Greek, or stood gaping like a fool when I was asked a question, the whole class rose to my defence and the teachers overlooked my faults. And yet in spite of this I gave up music.

I gave it up at the very moment when I had reason to feel that I was doing well and congratulations were pouring in on me. My divinity had returned; Scriabin had come back from Switzerland bringing his latest compositions including *L'Extase*. His arrival was a triumph and the whole of Moscow was celebrating his return. At the height of the festivities I called on him and played my pieces. His reaction surpassed all my hopes. He heard me out, approved, encouraged me and gave me his blessing.

But no one knew of my secret trouble and, had I spoken of it, I would not have been believed. I was getting on as a composer but I played wretchedly and I read music like a child learning to spell. The discrepancy between my musical themes, new and difficult in themselves, and my lack of practical skill turned the natural gift which should have been a joy to me into a torment, and in the end I found it unendurable.

How could this have come about? There was something basically wrong, something which called for retribution, in my attitude. I had the adolescent arrogance, the nihilist conceit of the half-taught which despises whatever seems attainable, whatever can be "earned" by effort. I looked down on industry as uncreative, taking it upon myself to lay down the law on matters of which I knew nothing. "In real life," I thought, everything must be miraculous and pre-ordained, nothing must be planned, deliberate, willed.

This was the negative side of Scriabin's influence on me. I took him for my supreme authority, not realising that he alone could afford his own egocentricity, that his teaching was right only for him. I misunderstood him childishly, but the seeds of his opinions had fallen on fertile soil.

I had always had mystical and superstitious leanings and a hankering after providential signs. Almost as far back as the night of the concert I had started to believe in a heroic world which claimed my joyful service although it was a source of anguish. How often, as a child of six, seven or eight, had I been close to suicide!

I suspected that all sorts of mysteries and lies surrounded me. There was no absurdity which I did not believe. At moments, at the dawn of life, the only moment when such foolishness is thinkable, I imagined (perhaps because I could remember my nurse dressing me in my first smocks) that I remembered having been a girl, and that I could regain this earlier more pleasing, more fascinating personality, by pulling in my belt so tight that I almost fainted. At other times I thought that I was not my parents' son but a foundling whom they had adopted.

So too, in my misfortunes as a musician, devious and imaginary causes were involved – oracles and signs and omens. I lacked perfect pitch. This was quite unnecessary to me in my work, but the discovery was a grief and a humiliation and I took it as proof that my music was rejected by heaven or fate. I had not the courage to stand up to all these blows and I lost heart.

For six years I had lived for music. Now I tore it up and flung it from me as you throw away your dearest treasure. For a while, I went on improvising by habit but I was gradually losing my skill. Then I decided to make a clean break – I stopped playing the piano or going to concerts, and I avoided meeting musicians.

Scriabin's defence of the superman was an expression of his native Russian craving for the superlative. Indeed, it is not only true that music needs to be more than itself if it is to mean anything, but that everything in the world must surpass itself in order to be itself. There must be something limitless in a human being and in his activity for either to have definition and character.

In view of my broken ties with music and of my failure to keep up with its developments, the Scriabin of my memories – the Scriabin who used to be my daily bread – is the Scriabin of his middle period, roughly between his third and fifth sonatas.[11]

To me, the Promethean lightnings[12] of his last works are not the daily food of the soul but merely added evidence of his genius, and of such evidence I have no need since I took him on trust from the beginning.

Men who have died young, such as Andrey Bely and Khlebnikov, spent the last years of their lives looking for a new means of expression, dreaming of a new language, groping for its vowels, consonants and syllables.

I have never understood the need for this kind of research. I believe the most astonishing discoveries of all to have been made at moments when the sense of his work so possessed the artist that it left him no time to think and he was driven by his urgency to speak new words in the old language, without stopping to know if it was old or new.

That was how Chopin, using the old idiom of Mozart and Field, said so many new things in music that he seems to be its new beginning.

And this was how Scriabin, very early on in his career and using almost nothing but the methods of his forerunners, changed and renovated the climate of music. As early as the Etudes of the Eighth Opus and the Preludes of the Eleventh, his work was already wholly contemporary, it had an inner correspondence, in musical terms, to the surrounding world, to the way people thought, felt, lived, dressed and travelled in those days.

The melodies in these compositions start as tears start to your eyes, and flow as tears flow from the corners of your eyes, down your cheeks to the corners of your mouth. They flow along your bare nerves and heart, and your tears are not tears of sorrow but of astonishment because the way into your heart has been so perfectly discovered.

All at once, there breaks into the flow of melody an answer to it, an objection in another, higher, feminine voice and in a simpler, conversational tone. The chance argument is resolved at once. But it leaves behind it the overwhelmingly disturbing note of that simplicity on which everything in art depends.

Art is full of generally accepted truths. But although their use is open to all, the well-known rules are hardly ever properly applied. A well-known truth needs special luck, the kind of luck that comes its way once in a century, to find its application. Scriabin was such a piece of luck. Just as Dostoyevsky was more than a mere novelist and Blok more than a mere poet, Scriabin was more than merely a composer – he is an everlasting reason for rejoicing and congratulation, a feast, a celebration in the history of Russian culture.

3. THE NINETEEN HUNDREDS

In answer to the student demonstrations which followed the Manifesto of 17 October,[1] the rabble of Okhotny Ryad[2] looted the University, some other colleges and the Higher Technical School. The College of Art was also threatened. By the Director's orders, piles of stones were kept on the landings of the main staircase and lengths of hose connected with the taps for use against possible raiders.

Every now and then, a crowd marching down our street turned aside and entered the building. Classrooms were occupied, meetings were held in the Assembly Hall, and from the balcony speakers addressed those who had remained in the street below. The College students joined the revolutionary paramilitary organisations and our own home guard was on duty at night.

Among my father's papers is a drawing of a girl speaking from the balcony; she is wounded and, supporting herself against a pillar, goes on speaking; dragoons are charging the crowd and shooting at her.

At the end of 1905, at the height of the general strike,[3] Gorky came back to Moscow. The nights were frosty; the pitch-black city was lit by bonfires. Stray bullets whistled down the empty streets, and mounted patrols charged with soundless fury over the untrodden snow.

My father saw Gorky several times in connection with the various new satirical papers, such as *The Scourge* and *The Bugaboo*[4] to whose editorial offices Gorky would invite him.

It was about that time, I think – though it may have been later, when we had returned to Moscow after a year's stay in Berlin[5] – that I came across a poem by Blok. I no longer remember what it was – perhaps the "Pussywillows" or something from *Childhood*[6] dedicated to Olenina d'Alheim, or something about the town and the revolution – but I remember my impression of it so distinctly that I am able to revive and to describe it now.

What do we usually mean by "literature"? A world of rhetoric, triteness, rounded phrases and respectable names, of those who have observed real life when they were young but who, once they have achieved fame, confine themselves to abstractions, to rehashing and to cautious common sense. Whenever, in this kingdom in which artificiality is so established that it goes unnoticed, anyone opens his mouth not out of a taste for verbal elegance but because he knows a thing and wants to say it, the result is an upheaval, as if the doors had been flung open and let in the noises of the street; not as if the speaker were reporting on events in town but as if the town itself were giving notice of its presence through his lips. This happened in the case of Blok; such was the effective power of his lonely, childlike, uncorrupted speech.

You looked at any one of his poems: it contained a piece of news. It seemed as if the piece of news had settled on the page of its own accord without anyone's permission, as if the poem had not been written down by anyone. What you saw was not a poem about wind and puddles and stars and street lamps, but the lamp-lit puddles rippling, wind-chased over the surface of the paper and leaving on it their strong, damp, disturbing trace.

Blok was part of my youth, as of the youth of others of my generation (I will speak of them later). He had all the qualities which go to make a great poet – passion, gentleness, dedicated insight, his own conception of the world, his own gift of transforming everything he touched, his own reserved, restrained, self-effacing destiny. Of all these qualities and many others besides, I will mention only one aspect – I found it the most striking and it therefore seemed to me predominant in him: his swiftness, his wandering yet attentive glance, the strange cursoriness of his observations.

> A light swung in the window.
> In the half-dark, alone,
> A harlequin whispered
> With the darkness at the porch
>
> The sweeping blizzard
> Swings up the streets:
> Somebody's hand reaches out to me
> And somebody else smiles.
>
> A teasing light waves,
> Blacks out like a face on a winter night
> When the silhouette of a shadow
> Slips through the doorway.[7]

Adjectives without a noun, predicates without a subject, alarm, excitement, hide-and-seek, abruptness, whisking shadows – how well this style accorded with the spirit of time, itself secretive, hermetic, underground, only just out of the cellars and still using the language of conspiracy, the spirit of a time and of a tale in which the chief character was the town and the street was the chief event.

These are the qualities which permeate the being of Blok, the essential and predominating Blok – the Blok of the second volume of the Alkonost edition, the author of *The Terrible World*, *The Last Day*, *Fraud*, *Story*, *Legend*, *Meeting*, *Stranger*, and the poems "In mist above the sparkling dew", "In taverns, alleys and lanes", and "A girl sang in the choir".[8]

Drawn by his perceptiveness, reality whirls into his poems like a stream of air. This is true of everything in his poetry, down to its apparent mysticism and "theology", which are not a form of metaphysical brooding but a scattering throughout his verse of torn fragments of the daily reality of churchgoing life – passages from litanies, communion prayers, burial psalms, versicles which he knew by heart through having heard them hundreds of times in church.

The sum, the heart, the bearer of all this reality was the city, the Petersburg of his poems – for Petersburg was the real hero of his story, the subject of his biography.

Of all the Petersburgs conceived by artists of our time, his is the most real. It is indistinguishably the same in imagination and in life; it is full of the prose of its daily round, the prose which communicates drama and unrest to poetry, and the language spoken in its streets is the current language of colloquial conversation by which poetic language is refreshed.

And yet the features of this portrait of a town are drawn by so sensitive a hand and are so spiritualised, that the whole of it is also the absorbing image of a most remarkable inner world.

I had been lucky enough to get to know many of the older poets who lived in Moscow[9] but I was only introduced to Blok when he came to Moscow for the last time.[10] It was on the night of a poetry reading at the Polytechnical Museum: I met him on the stairs or on the landing outside the lecture hall. He was very friendly; he said that he had heard nothing but good of me and would like to know me, but that he was feeling ill that evening and would have to put off seeing me until he was better.

That evening he was to read poetry in three different places – at the Polytechnic, at the Press Club, and at the Dante Society where an enthusiastic audience of his followers was awaiting him to hear his "Italian Poems".

Mayakovsky whom I met at the Polytechnic told me that a plot had been cooked up at the Press Club and that, under the pretext of independent criticism, Blok was to be received with catcalls, whistles and abuse. Mayakovsky suggested that we should go there and try to prevent this infamy.

We set off immediately, but, since we went on foot, while Blok, as soon as he had finished at the Polytechnic, was taken by car, it was all over by the time we reached the club in the Nikitsky Boulevard. Blok had already left for the Dante Society. The row had been as bad as we had feared. After the reading, insults had been showered on him; he was even told to his face that he was a "back number" and a "living corpse"; with all of this he quietly agreed. And all of this was said to him a few months before his death.[11]

In those years of our first experiments only two poets of our generation possessed the mastery of an accomplished and mature poetic style: they were Aseyev and Tsvetayeva. As for the rest of us, our boasted originality, including mine, came from our complete and helpless inarticulateness, which did not prevent us from writing, publishing and translating verse. Of all the depressing and incompetent pieces I wrote at that time the most horrible were my translations of Ben Jonson's *Alchemist* and of Goethe's *Mysteries*.[12] Blok reviewed my version of *Mysteries* for the publishers of *World Literature* and the review was afterwards included with others in the last volume of his Collected Works. Its crushingly contemptuous tone was just and well deserved. But I have run ahead of my story and must go back to where I left it, far back in the early nineteen hundreds.

When I was in my third or fourth form at school, I spent the Christmas holidays in Petersburg.[13] My uncle, who was head of the Petersburg goods station on the Nikolayevsky Line, gave me a warrant and I travelled up by myself by train. All day long I wandered about the streets of the immortal city, as if my eyes and feet were devouring some work of genius in stone; I spent my evenings at Komissarzhevskaya's Theatre.[14] I was intoxicated by the latest books; I raved about Andrey Bely, Hamsun, Przybyszewski.

An even wider, more genuine experience of travelling was our journey to Berlin where we all went in 1906. For the first time in my life I was abroad.

Everything was unusual, different from what it was at

home. It was less like living than like dreaming, or like taking part in some improvisation on the stage, some entertainment without rules, which no one had a duty to take part in or attend. There was nobody you knew, nobody to lay down the law to you – doors flapping open and shut in an endless row along the lane of carriages – each compartment with its separate door. Four tracks curving along a circular viaduct overlooking the gigantic city, high above its streets, canals, racing stables and back yards. Trains chasing and overtaking one another, running side by side and separating. Street lights dividing, intersecting under railway bridges; lights in first and second storey windows, level with the tracks; jewelled clusters of pin-point illumination on slot machines in station restaurants (the slot machines threw out cigars, chocolates and sugared almonds). I was soon familiar with Berlin, loafing about in its countless streets and in its endless park, breathing its mixture of gas, train smoke and beer fumes, talking German with a fake *Berliner* accent and listening to Wagner.

Berlin was full of Russians. The composer Rebikov played his "Christmas Tree" for his friends and explained that there were three periods in music: bestial until Beethoven, human between Beethoven and Rebikov, and the music of the future.

Gorky too was in Berlin.[15] My father made a drawing of him. Andreyeva disliked it: the cheekbones were too prominent so that the face looked angular. She said: "You haven't understood him. He is Gothic." That was how they spoke in those days.

It must have been soon after our return to Moscow that another great contemporary lyric poet came into my life; this was the German, Rainer Maria Rilke,[16] who was hardly known in those days but who is now recognised by the whole world.

In 1900 he had been to see Tolstoy at Yasnaya Polyana. He had spent one summer with the peasant poet Drozhzin in the country, at Zavidovo, near Klin, and he knew and corresponded with my father.

In those far-off days when his early poems were being published, he sent my father copies of his books inscribed with friendly dedications. Two such books happened to fall into my hands that winter, long after they had arrived. They shook me by the same insistent, unconditional gravity, the same directness in the use of language as had first astonished me in Blok.

In Russia Rilke is unknown. The few translations of him have been unsuccessful. The translators are not to blame. They are used to conveying meaning but not tone, and in Rilke tone is everything.

I had no idea of his reputation abroad until one day in 1913, when Verhaeren, who was in Moscow, was sitting for his portrait. My father asked me, as he did sometimes, to amuse his model so that his expression should not grow set and lifeless. In this way I had had to entertain the historian Klyuchevsky. Now it was Verhaeren. Needless to say I was a great admirer of his work and spoke to him about it; then I asked him diffidently if he had ever heard of Rilke. I could not imagine that he actually knew him. Verhaeren was transfigured. My father could not have asked for anything better than the change in his expression at the mere sound of Rilke's name. "He is the best poet in Europe," said Verhaeren, "and my beloved sworn brother."

Unlike Blok, who regarded prose as the source of poetry but who did not integrate it in his own writing, Rilke looked on the descriptive and psychological discoveries of the novelists of his time (Tolstoy, Flaubert, Proust and the Scandinavians) as intimately linked with his own poetic language and style.

However, I could go on describing and analysing him for ever without giving any clear impression of his work unless I gave an example.[17]

It was in about 1907 that a crop of new publishers sprang up like mushrooms, modern compositions were performed at many concerts, and art exhibitions opened one after another – "The World of Art", "The Golden Fleece", "The Knave of Diamonds", "The Donkey's Tail", "The Blue Rose".[18] Among the many Russian names – Somov, Sapunov, Sudeykin, Krymov, Laryonov, Goncharova – flickered the names of Frenchmen – Bonnard, Vuillard. Pictures by Matisse and sculptures by Rodin arrived from Paris and could be seen at The Golden Fleece, in darkly curtained halls which smelled of mould like hot-houses, so crowded were they with pots of hyacinths. Many young people joined the new artistic movements.

An old wooden house still stood in the courtyard of one of the new blocks of flats in Razgulyay Square. The owner lived in it; he was a general. On the top floor the General's son, the poet and painter Julian Anisimov, gathered round him a circle of young people who shared his interests. He had a weak chest and spent the winter abroad, but on fine evenings in spring and autumn he gave parties at which there were reading, music, sketching, arguments, and tea laced with rum. There I met a great many people.

The host, a most gifted being, a man of excellent taste, well read and cultivated, speaking several languages as fluently as Russian, was the embodiment of that poetic quality which gives charm to the amateur but is difficult to combine with a strong creative personality or the character of a master craftsman. We had many favourites and interests in common. I liked him very much.

It was at Anisimov's that I met Sergey Durylin, who has since died; at that time he was writing under the pseudonym of Sergey Rayevsky. In his kindness he managed to see something worthy of attention in my first experiments and it was under his influence that I was finally won over from music to writing. He lived in great poverty, keeping his mother and his aunt by giving lessons, and his ardent integ-

integrity and fanatical convictions recalled the figure of Belinsky as it is handed down to us by legend.

It was also at Anisimov's that Loks, whom I already knew – he was my fellow student at the University – first made me read Innokenty Annensky, a remarkable poet until then unknown to me, between whose work and my scribblings and wanderings Loks had established an imaginary kinship.

Our circle had a name. It had been christened "Serdarda"; none of us knew what this meant. It was understood that Arkady Guryev, a poet and singer and a member of the circle, had once heard it on the Volga. He heard it at night, in the confusion which inevitably happens when two boats arrive almost simultaneously at a landing stage: the two are lashed side by side, and the passengers of the second arrival go ashore with their luggage through the bowels of the first, and get entangled with its passengers and all their things.

Guryev came from Saratov. He had a deep, gentle, powerful voice and the art of bringing out every tonal and dramatic subtlety of anything he sang. Like most rough diamonds,[19] he astonished one as much by his incessant fooling as by the depth and genuineness which showed occasionally through his affectation. His verse was well above the average, and our delight in it foreshadowed our delight in Mayakovsky's unbridled sincerity and in Yesenin's clear-cut images, conveyed in all their freshness to the reader. An accomplished operatic singer and dramatic artist, he was that very essence of the born actor which Ostrovsky has portrayed so often.

He had a head as round as an onion with a big forehead, a nose that hardly showed at all and a bald patch which promised to spread from brow to nape. He was all movement, all expression. He never gestured with his hands, but as he stood arguing or reciting his whole body moved, acted, spoke. Torso thrown back, head sideways, legs wide apart, he looked as if he had been struck motionless in the middle of a Russian dance. He was prone, a little, to drinking bouts, and when drunk he would start believing his own nonsense. At the end of a turn he would pretend that his foot was stuck to the floor and assure us that the devil had him by the heel.

To the Serdarda came poets and painters, Krasin who had set Blok's "Pussywillows" to music; Bobrov whose early poems were published with mine and whose appearance in Razgulyay was preceded by his reputation as a newly-hatched Russian Rimbaud; Kozhebatkin, the editor of *Musaget*[20]; and, when he was in Moscow, Sergey Makovsky, the editor of *Apollo*.

I joined the Serdarda on the strength of my reputation as a musician; as the guests arrived I improvised musical sketches of each of them.

The short spring night was soon over. The cold morning breathed through the open windows. Its breath lifted the hems of the curtains, stirred the flame of the guttering candles and rustled the papers scattered on the table. We all yawned – host, guests, the empty distance, the grey sky, the rooms, the stairs. Finally we went home along the wide streets which seemed longer through being empty, overtaking as we went the procession of rattling cesspool carts. "Centaurs," one of us would say in the idiom of the time.

A sort of school grew up around the *Musaget*. Writers and critics[21] lectured to eager young people on poetic rhythm, the history of German romanticism, Russian lyric poetry, the æsthetics of Goethe and Richard Wagner; Baudelaire and the French symbolists, and pre-Socratic Greek philosophy.

The heart and soul of all this activity was Andrey Bely, the unchallenged leader of the movement. He was a first-rate poet and even more remarkable as the prose-writer of the *Symphonies* and of the two novels *The Silver Dove* and *Petersburg*, which transformed pre-revolutionary Russian taste and were the starting point of Soviet prose.

Bely had all the marks of genius – it was a genius which, unharnessed by daily difficulties, family life or the incomprehension of his friends, raced in a vacuum and had turned from a creative power into a barren and destructive force. This failing which arose from an excess of spirituality did not lower him in our eyes but gained our sympathy and added to his attraction a note of suffering.

He gave a practical course on Russian iambic verse and in discussion with his students used statistics to explain its rhythmic figures and variations. I took no part in these discussions for I believed then, as I still do now, that verbal music is not a matter of acoustics or of harmonising vowels and consonants as such, but of relating sound to meaning.

One of the places where the young enthusiasts of the *Musaget* occasionally gathered was the studio of the sculptor Krakht in the Presnya district.

Half-way up the walls there was a gallery which Krakht used as his bedroom; below it on the floor, white among the decorative plants and draping ivy, were clay masks, casts of antique fragments and his own works.

One evening in the late autumn I went to Krakht's to read a paper on "Symbolism and Immortality". Part of the audience sat on the floor, the rest lay on the floor of the gallery hanging their heads over the edge.

My thesis was based on the idea that our impressions are subjective, that there is a difference between the sounds and colours we perceive and the corresponding sound and light vibrations which exist objectively in the world around us. I developed the idea that these subjective impressions and the capacity to receive them are not an attribute of the separate individual but are suprapersonal and racial, the common property of the world of man, of the human race. I assumed that every human being leaves behind him when he dies his own share of this undying, racial subjectivity – the share contained in him in his lifetime and which enabled him to take part in human history. My purpose was to suggest that in this ultimate, subjective and yet universal area of the soul, art finds its everlasting field of action and its main content; and that although the artist is of course mortal like everyone else, the joy of living experienced by him is immortal and can be felt by others through his work, centuries after his death, in a form approximating to that of his original, intimately personal experience.

The paper was called "Symbolism and Immortality" because it maintained that, in the sense in which it is possible to speak of symbols in algebra, all art is in essence conventional and symbolic.

The audience was interested and the discussion which followed went on late into the night. When I got home I heard that Tolstoy, who had left his home at Yasnaya Polyana and collapsed at the railway station of Astapovo, had died.[22] Father had been summoned to Astapovo by telegram. We went off at once to catch the night train from Paveletsky Station.

In those days the difference between town and country was greater than it is now, the transition as you left town was more abrupt. From early morning onwards, the same endless view of ploughed or fallow land, hardly varied by scattered villages, filled the carriage window: this was the thousand mile expanse of Russian peasant countryside which laboured for and fed the small urban Russia of that time. The fields were already silvered by the first frosts and were still framed along their boundaries by the gold remaining on the birch trees; and these modest ornaments of hoar-frost silver and birch-tree gold lay upon the land like the gold and silver-leaf illumination of its holy and meek antiquity.

The land resting, ploughed or fallow, flickered outside the window, knowing nothing of the death, nearby, of the last of her giants. A man fit by birth to be her tsar and the sophistication of whose mind, surfeited by all the refinements of the world, could have made him the favourite among all favourites, the lordling among lordlings, but who, for love of her and out of scrupulous concern for her, had instead followed the plough, dressed and belted like a peasant.

*

Those who had been taking leave of Tolstoy's body had probably been asked to wait outside while a drawing of him and then a death mask were being made (Merkurov had brought a caster). We came into an empty room. Then Sofya Andreyevna[23] rose and came forward hurriedly from the far corner; she clutched my father's hands and spoke feverishly through her tears: "Oh, what I have been through, Leonid Osipovich! You know how much I loved him," and she went on to tell Father how, when Tolstoy left home, she had tried to drown herself and was dragged half dead out of the lake.

Tolstoy's presence filled the room like a mountain – say like Elbrus – or like a storm cloud the size of half a sky. And Tolstoy's widow was as much a part of it as a great cliff taken from the mountain or as lightning flashing from the cloud. But she did not know that she had the right of cliffs and lightning to be silent and unaccountable in her acts; that she need not enter into argument with the Tolstoyans who had less in common with Tolstoy than anyone in the world; that she had only to ignore their pigmy challenge.[24]

So she justified herself and called upon my father to bear witness that her devotion to her husband and her understanding of his mind were greater than her rivals', and that she could have taken better care of him than they did. God, I thought, how can anyone – let alone Tolstoy's wife – be reduced to this!

It really is strange! A modern critic with an up-to-date outlook, who condemns duelling in general as an antiquated custom, has published an enormous work on Pushkin's duel and his death.[25] Poor Pushkin! Why didn't he marry Shchegolev and modern Pushkinology? Then everything would have been in order. He would still be alive to-day, and he would have written several sequels to *Evgeny Onegin* and five *Poltavas* instead of one. My own feeling has always been that I would not understand a word of Pushkin if I admitted for a moment that he needed our understanding of him more than he needed his wife.[26]

*

But what there was in the far corner of the room was not a mountain but a wrinkled little old man, one of the dozens of old men invented by Tolstoy and scattered through his books. The place bristled with fir saplings which stood round the bed, their outlines sharpened by the setting sun. Four slanting sheaves of light reached across the room and threw over the corner where the body lay the sign of the big shadow of the crosspiece of the window and the small, childish crosses of the shadows of the firs.

That day the station of Astapovi had turned into the braying camp of the world Press. Trade was brisk at the station restaurant. Waiters were run off their feet, hardly able to keep up with orders and galloping with plates of rare beef steaks. Beer flowed like a river.

Waiting at the station were Tolstoy's sons Ilya and Andrey. Sergey was on the train which came to fetch Tolstoy's body and take it to Yasnaya Polyana.

Students and young people, singing "Eternal Memory", bore the coffin across the small station yard, the garden and the platform to the waiting train and put it in the guard's van. The mourners who crowded on the platform bared their heads, and to the sound of renewed singing the train moved slowly in the direction of Tula.

It was somehow natural that Tolstoy should have found his rest and found it by the wayside like a pilgrim, close to one of Russia's railways on which his heroes and heroines continued to fly past and round and round, unaware, as they glanced out of the carriage window and caught sight of the small station, that here the eyes which had seen them, embraced them, and immortalised them had closed for ever.

If every writer were to be described by only one of his outstanding qualities – as we might speak of the passionate quality of Lermontov, of Tyutchev's fecundity of thought, of Chekhov's poetry, of Gogol's dazzling brilliance, or of the power of Dostoyevsky's imagination – what should we then say of Tolstoy?

Tolstoy was a moralist, a leveller, a preacher of a system of justice applicable to every human being without exception and in equal measure; yet the most outstanding of his qualities was his unique originality – an originality which goes to the point of paradox.

Throughout all his life he could always look at an event and see the whole of it, in the isolated, self-contained finality of its moment, as a vivid and exhaustive sketch – see it as the rest of us can only see on rare occasions, in childhood, or at a crest of happiness which renews the world, or in the joy of some great victory of the soul.

To have this vision the eye needs to be directed by passion. It is the flaring up of passion that illuminates the object and intensifies its visibility.

Such a passion – the passion of creative contemplation – Tolstoy bore incessantly within himself. And it was in its light that he could see each thing in its primordial freshness, in a new way and as though for the first time. The genuineness of his vision is so outside our normal habits that it may strike us as strange. But he did not look for this strangeness, he did not pursue it as an aim, still less did he use it as a literary method.[27]

4 EVE OF THE FIRST
WORLD WAR

I spent the spring and summer of 1912 abroad. Our summer vacations coincide with the summer term in Western universities; I spent it at the ancient University of Marburg.

It was there that Lomonosov had studied under the great mathematician and philosopher Christian Wolff; and there, a century and a half earlier, Giordano Bruno had broken his return journey to Rome to read a paper on his new system of astronomy before going home – and to his death at the stake.

Marburg was a small and picturesque medieval town. In those days it had a population of twenty-nine thousand; half were students. Moulded into the contours of a hill where the stone of its houses, churches, universities and castle had been quarried, it was sunk deep in gardens as dark as night.

At the end of the term I had a few pennies left of the sum provided for my studies and my keep in Germany; I used them to go on to Italy. I saw Venice, brick rose and aquamarine like the transparent pebbles on a beach, and Florence, dark, beautiful, cooped up, snatched bodily out of Dante; I ran out of money before I could visit Rome.[1]

In the following year I took my degree at the University of Moscow. Mansurov, a young historian who had stayed on at the University as a post-graduate, lent me a mass of books which he had used in preparing for his own examinations the year before. There was more than enough in his professorial library to satisfy the examiners – not only general text books but detailed reference works on classical antiquities and monographs on special subjects. I could hardly get all this wealth into a cab when I took it home.

Mansurov had two friends who were also his kinsmen, young Nikolay Trubetskoy and Dmitry Samarin. I had known them at school where they came to sit for their end of year examinations although they worked the rest of the time at home.

There were two older Trubetskoys teaching at the University; Nikolay's father held the Chair of general theory of Law, while his uncle, a well-known philosopher, was the Rector. Both of them remarkably stout, they lumbered on to the dais like elephants dressed up in waistless coats, and delivered their splendid lectures in imploring accents and in droning, whining voices with an aristocratic rhotacism.[2]

The three young people had a family look. Tall, gifted youths, with eyebrows joined together in a single line and voices as resounding as their names, they dropped in at the university as an inseparable trio.

The Marburg philosophical school[3] was greatly honoured in their circle. Trubetskoy's uncle wrote about it and encouraged his most promising students to attend its courses. Samarin who had been to them before me was at home in Marburg and a Marburg patriot, and it was on his advice that I went there myself.

Samarin came from a famous Slavophil family;[4] they had a property near Moscow, on which the Writers' Settlement of Peredelkino[5] and the Peredelkino Tuberculosis Sanatorium for children stand to-day.

Philosophy, dialectics and Hegelian scholarship were in Samarin's blood as a hereditary gift. He was disorderly, absent-minded and almost certainly a little mad. The eccentricities which startled his friends when the mood was on him made him impossible to live with. He was always quarrelling with his relations and they could not be blamed for falling out with him.

At the beginning of the NEP[6] Samarin, dishevelled,

35

stripped of sophistication and full of all-forgiving understanding, came back to Moscow from Siberia where the Civil
War had tossed him to and fro for a long time. He was
swollen with hunger and covered with lice from his journey.
He caught typhus and died towards the end of the epidemic.

The fate of Mansurov is unknown to me. The philologist,
Nikolay Trubetskoy, achieved a world-wide reputation and
has died recently in Vienna.

After my finals I spent the summer[7] at my parents' *dacha* in
Molodi, near the station of Stolbovaya on the Moscow-Kursk
railway.

According to tradition, Cossaks who were part of our
retreating army had used the house as a snipers' nest against
the forward units of Napoleon. Their graves, sunk and over-
grown, could still be seen in the graveyard at the far end of
the park.

The rooms were narrow in proportion to their height
and had tall windows. At night the oil-lamp threw gigantic
shadows on the ceiling and the dark, Bordeaux-coloured
walls.

At the bottom of the park there was a narrow winding
stream with many deep eddies and, leaning over it almost
upside down, an old birch tree, half up-rooted but still
growing.

The thick green tangle of its branches hanging in mid-air
above the water made a natural summer-house; you could
lie or sit in it in comfort. I made it my work-room.

I read Tyutchev and, for the first time in my life, wrote
poetry not as a rare exception but regularly, every day, as
people paint or compose music.

Perched in my tree, I wrote all the poems for my first book
in those two or three summer months.

With stupid pretentiousness, I called the book *Twin in the
Clouds*; this was in imitation of the cosmological obscurities
of the book-titles of the symbolists and of the imprints of their
publishers.

To write these poems – to scribble, to scratch out and to restore the vanished lines – this was my deepest need and my joy, a joy which nothing else could give me and which moved me to tears.

I did my best to avoid poetic coquetry.[8] I felt no need to thunder my verses from a platform and make the hair rise on the heads of intellectuals with indignation at their "barbarism" and "vulgarity"; nor to read them to a closed circle of a chosen few who would congratulate me on my "integrity", nor to make highbrow ladies swoon with rapture at their discreet refinement. Nor was I trying to achieve a song or dance-tune rhythm, so marked and jolly that it sets the arms and legs of hearers jigging almost without help from words. I was not expressing or reflecting or portraying or reacting against anything.

It was only later, when an attempt was made to establish a resemblance between Mayakovsky and myself, that I was credited with a gift for tonal and rhetorical effects. This is quite untrue – I have no more of this gift than anyone who uses words.

On the contrary, my concern has always been for meaning, and my dream that every poem should have content in itself – a new thought or a new image. And that the whole of it with all its individual character should be engraved so deeply into the book that it should speak from it with all the silence and with all the colours of its colourless black print.

Thus I wrote a poem called "Venice", and another called "The Railway Station". What I saw before me as I was writing was the town standing on the water, the figures-of-eight and circles of its reflections drifting, multiplying, swelling like a biscuit soaked in tea. Or the distance of the railway station, where the tracks and platforms end in clouds and smoke and the trains vanish, and the skyline of departure ends the history of situations – meetings and farewells and events before and after them.

I was concerned neither with myself nor with my readers nor with the theory of art. All I cared about was that one poem should contain the town of Venice, and the other the Brest (now called the Byelorussian-Baltic) railway station.

Bobrov liked the lines, "The shifts of trains and of misfortunes would unfold the West."[9] He and Aseyev with several beginners like myself had started a small publishing firm on a co-operative basis. Bobrov who had a knowledge of typography from having worked for *Russian Archive*[10] produced his own books and ours. He published my *Twin* with a friendly introduction by Aseyev.

The wife of the poet Baltrushaytis told me that it was immature and that some day I would be sorry I had brought it out. I have indeed often regretted it.[11]

I was staying with the Baltrushaytis family in the hot summer of '14, the summer of the drought and of the total eclipse of the sun. This was on a big estate on the Oka[12] near the town of Alexin. I gave lessons to his son and worked on a translation of Kleist's comedy, *The Broken Jug*; it had been commissioned by the newly founded Studio Theatre[13] to which Baltrushaytis acted as literary adviser.

Nearby, at Tarusa, Balmont was translating Kalidasa's *Shakuntala* for the same Studio Theatre, and several other people connected with the arts lived on the estate – the poet Vyacheslav Ivanov, the painter Ulyanov and the wife of the writer Muratov.

In July I went to Moscow for my call-up, but was exempted because my riding accident as a child had left me with one leg shorter than the other.

One evening soon after my return to the country there was a curious happening on the Oka. For a long time we heard some kind of regimental music – marching songs and polkas – drifting slowly towards us down the river, but we could see nothing but the low mist clinging to the reeds. Then a small steam tug nosed its way round a promontory with three barges in tow. The people on the boat must have caught sight of the house on the hill and decided to land, for the tug turned, cut across the stream and pulled the barges over to our bank. We saw then that there were soldiers on them – a large contingent of Grenadiers. The men came ashore and lit camp-fires at the bottom of the hill. The officers were asked up to the house to dine and spend the night. Next morning they all sailed away. This was one of the incidents of the advance mobilisation. A few days later the war broke out.

After this I spent almost a year – two stretches with several breaks – as tutor to the son of a rich merchant, Morritz Philipp;[14] my pupil, Walter, was a charming and affectionate boy.

In the summer, when there were anti-German demonstrations and raiders broke into the premises of several big German firms such as Einem's and Ferrein's,[15] Philipp's office and his private house were wrecked and looted.

The raids were carried out according to plan and with the knowledge of the police. Only the property of the employers was supposed to suffer, that of the people they employed was left untouched. Most of my belongings, including all my clothes, were spared, but in the confusion my books and manuscripts got into the general chaos and were destroyed.

Later, I lost many of my manuscripts in more peaceful circumstances. I do not like my own style before 1940, just as I quarrel with half of Mayakovsky's writings and with some of Yesenin's. The disintegration of forms, the impoverishment of thought and the littered and uneven style, then general, are alien to me. I have no regrets for the faulty works I lost. For quite a different reason I do not regret the loss of my successful writings either.

It is more important in life to lose than to acquire. Unless the seed dies it bears no fruit. One must live tirelessly, looking to the future, and drawing upon those reserves of life which are created not only by remembrance but also by forgetting.

At various times and for various reasons I have lost my paper on "Symbolism and Immortality", several articles written in my futuristic period, a fairytale for children in prose, two poems, a note-book of verse which should have come between *Above the Barriers* and *My Sister, Life*, several foolscap note-books containing a rough draft of a novel (except for the first chapter which I revised and published as a story, *The Childhood of Luvers*) and the translation of one whole tragedy from Swinburne's trilogy on Mary Stuart.

The Philipps moved from their half-burned and looted house into a furnished flat. I went with them. I remember my room. The rays of the setting autumn sun furrowed the room and the book of which I turned the pages. The evening was reflected as a pale pink bloom upon the pages of the book. And evening, in another of its aspects, was the heart, the matter of the poems it contained. I envied the simplicity of the author's means and the reality which they had netted. It was one of Akhmatova's early works, probably her *Plantain*.[16]

In the intervals of coaching Walter, I stayed in the Urals and in the Kama district. I spent a winter in Vsevolodo-Vilva, north of Perm, once visited by Chekhov and by Levitan, according to the memoirs of A. N. Tikhonov who describes it. Another winter I spent in the Tikhy Mountains working in the Ushkovs' chemical factory near the Kama.[17]

For some time I was responsible for examining the cases of men of military age whose work at the factory was a reserved occupation, and I released whole townships of potential recruits.

In winter the Urals factories kept in touch with the outside world by prehistoric methods of communication. The mail was carried from Kazan, a distance of two hundred miles,[18] by troika as in the days of the Captain's daughter.[19] I once made this journey.

In March 1917 the news of the outbreak of the revolution in Petersburg reached the factory and I went to Moscow.

My first stop was to be at the Izhevsk works[20] where I had to pick up the engineer Zbarsky, a remarkable man, to put myself under his orders and continue the journey with him.

All night and part of the next day we raced down from

the Tikhy Mountains in a small covered wagon on sleighs. Muffled in three sheepskins and smothered in hay, I rolled helplessly from side to side at the bottom of the wagon like a sack. I dozed, slept and woke up, opened and closed my eyes.

I could see the forest road and the stars in the frosty night. Tall snowdrifts humped the narrow track like hills. Often, the wagon caught the lower branches of the overhanging pines, scattering their snow and scratching along them as it rustled noisily underneath. The starlight was reflected in the whiteness of the sheet of snow and lit the way. The shining pall of snow was frightening in the deep thickness of the woods, as if a burning candle had been set into the forest.

The three horses raced in single file, harnessed head to tail, now one now another swerving out of line; the coachman kept pulling them in, and when the wagon keeled over he jumped out and ran alongside, propping it with his shoulder to keep it from overturning.

Again I slept, losing consciousness of time, and was aroused suddenly by a jolt and the cessation of movement.

The coaching station in the forest was like a camp of robbers in a fairytale. A light glimmered in a hut. A clock ticked and a samovar simmered. While the coachman who had brought the wagon undid his things and warmed himself, talking with the woman who was getting him supper in a quiet, night-time voice, not to disturb whoever was asleep the other side of the partition, the new coachman wiped his lips and his moustache, buttoned up his coat and went out into the frost to harness the new troika.

And again the horses raced, the sleigh whistled over the snow and I dozed and slept. Then, the next day, there were factory chimneys in the distance, the limitless snow desert of a vast frozen river, and a railway track.

Bobrov treated me with undeserved warmth. He watched ceaselessly over my integrity as a futurist and kept me from all harmful influences. By these he understood the sympathy of my elders. Lest their kindness should lead me into academic ways, he rushed in the moment he saw the least sign of anyone taking an interest in me and obliged me, by whatever means, to break off the dangerous connection he had noted. Thanks to him I was always breaking with someone.

I liked Julian Anisimov and his wife Vera Stanevich. Bobrov dragged me into his quarrel with them and I lost their friendship.

Vyacheslav Ivanov wrote a touching dedication in the copy which he gave me of his book. Bobrov made fun of it in Bryusov's circle, in such a way that I seemed to have put him up to it. Next time he saw me, Vyacheslav Ivanov cut me dead.

A periodical, *The Contemporary*,[21] printed my translation of Kleist's comedy, *The Broken Jug*. My work was immature and dull. I ought to have been humbly grateful to the periodical for printing it, and still more grateful to the unknown editor who had revised it, greatly to its benefit.

But modesty, gratitude, sense of truth, were not in currency among the young artistic circles of the left; such feelings were considered mawkish. The proper thing was to be insolent and strut about sticking one's nose up in the air, and although it sickened me, I tagged along not to be left behind.

Something went wrong with the proofs of my translation. I got them late and compositors' notes somehow came to be included in the text.

Bobrov, to do him justice, had no idea of what was going on and, on this occasion, really did not know what he was doing. He said the whole thing was a disgrace – both the printer's errors and the unasked-for corrections of the style of the manuscript: I couldn't possibly let it pass. I must complain to Gorky; Bobrov had heard that he was somehow unofficially connected with the magazine. I followed his advice. Instead of thanking the board of *The Contemporary* I wrote Gorky an idiotic letter, full of ignorance, conceit and affectation, complaining of what in fact had been the kindness and consideration they had shown me. Years passed, and I discovered that I had complained to Gorky about Gorky. The manuscript had been printed on his instructions and it was he who had corrected it with his own hand.

Even my first meeting with Mayakovsky was the result of an encounter between two rival futurist groups; he belonged to one and I to the other. The organisers had counted on a row, but the difficulty was that our mutual understanding became obvious from our first words.

I will not speak of my relations with Mayakovsky at length.[22] Our friendship was never close. His account of it has been exaggerated; his judgments of my work have been distorted. He disliked *Nineteen Five* and *Lieutenant Schmidt* and thought that I ought never to have written them; he liked two of my books, *Above the Barriers* and *My Sister, Life*.

I won't go into the history of our agreements and disagreements. I will only try, so far as possible, to give a general impression of Mayakovsky and of his significance. Naturally, it will be partial and subjectively coloured.

To start with the most important: We have no conception of the inner torture which precedes suicide. People who are physically tortured on the rack keep losing consciousness, their suffering is so great that its unendurable intensity shortens the end. But a man who is thus at the mercy of the executioner is not annihilated when he faints from pain, for he is present at his own end, his past belongs to him, his memories are his and, if he chooses, he can make use of them, they can help him before his death.

But a man who decides to commit suicide puts a full stop to his being, he turns his back on his past, he declares himself a bankrupt and his memories to be unreal. They can no longer help or save him, he has put himself beyond their reach. The continuity of his inner life is broken, his personality is at an end. And perhaps what finally makes him kill himself is not the firmness of his resolve but the unbearable quality of this anguish which belongs to no one, of this

43

suffering in the absence of the sufferer, of this waiting which
is empty because life has stopped and can no longer fill it.

It seems to me that Mayakovsky shot himself out of pride,
because he condemned something in himself, or close to him,
to which his self-respect could not submit. That Yesenin
hanged himself without having properly thought out the
consequences of his act, still saying in his inmost heart:
"Who knows? Perhaps this isn't yet the end. Nothing is yet
decided." That Marina Tsvetayeva had always held her
work between herself and the reality of daily life; and when
she found this luxury beyond her means, when she felt that
for her son's sake she must, for a time, give up her passionate
absorption in poetry and looked round her soberly, she saw
chaos, no longer screened by art, fixed, unfamiliar, motionless, and, not knowing where to run for terror, she hid in
death, putting her neck into the noose as she might have
hidden her head under her pillow. It seems to me that Paolo
Yashvili was utterly confused, spellbound by the Shi-
galyovshchina[23] of 1937 as by witchcraft; and that he
watched his daughter as she slept at night and, imagining
himself unworthy to look at her, went out in the morning to
his friends' house and blasted his head with grapeshot from
his double-barrelled gun. And it seems to me that Fadeyev,
still with the apologetic smile which had somehow stayed
with him through all the crafty ins and outs of politics, told
himself just before he pulled the trigger: "Well, now it's all
over. Good-bye, Sasha."[24]

What is certain is that they all suffered beyond description,
to the point where suffering has become a mental sickness.
And, as we bow in homage to their gifts and to their
bright memory, we should bow compassionately before their
suffering.

But to come back to the summer of 1914 and to the coffee-
house in the Arbat[25] where it was intended that our two
literary factions should clash. Bobrov and I had been sent
to represent our side; Tretyakov and Shershenevich, who

represented theirs, brought Mayakovsky with them.

It turned out that I knew him by sight. We had been to the same school, though he had been my junior by two years,[26] and I had also seen him at concerts.

A few days earlier a man who was later to become one of his blind followers showed me some newly published verses of Mayakovsky's. So little did this future disciple understand his god at the time that he laughed at them and was indignant as at an obvious piece of giftless nonsense. But the poem had attracted me immensely. It was one of his most brilliant early experiments, and was afterwards included in *As Simple as Mooing*.[27]

Now, at the café, I found that I liked the author no less than I had liked his verse. Before me sat a handsome, sombre youth with a boxer's fists, the deep voice of an Archdeacon and an inexhaustible, deadly wit – something between one of Alexander Grin's mythical heroes and a Spanish toreador.

He was handsome, witty, talented – perhaps even super-latively talented, but you knew at once that these were not the most important things about him; the important thing was his iron mastery over himself, the rules or principles of honour, the sense of duty which prevented him from being any different, any less handsome, talented or witty than he was.

His resolute expression and the mane of hair which stood on end as he ruffled it with all five fingers, immediately reminded me of some young terrorist conspirator out of a Dostoyevsky novel, some minor Dostoyevsky character from the provinces.

It was not always to their disadvantage that the provinces lagged behind the capitals. In periods when the great cities fell into decline, the far-out regions were sometimes rescued by the survival in them of their virtuous past. Thus, into the kingdom of the tango and of skating rinks, Mayakovsky had brought from the remote forests of Transcaucasia where he was born the conviction, still unshaken in that forgotten corner of the world, that enlightenment in Russia could only be revolutionary.

To his natural advantages he added an artistic disorder, draped himself in a certain rough and careless clumsiness of mind and body and assuming the role of a bohemian rebel, which he acted with supreme taste. His taste was so experienced and mature that it seemed older than himself. He was twenty-two while his taste was at least a hundred and twenty-two.

I was very fond of Mayakovsky's early lyrics. Against the contemporary background of affectation and fooling, their gravity – heavy, menacing, complaining – stood out remarkably. It was poetry moulded by a master; proud and dæmonic and at the same time infinitely doomed, at the point of death, almost an appeal for help.

> Time, I beg: though you are a lame dauber of holy
>   images
> Daub my likeness into the tabernacle of our misshapen
>   age.
> I am as lonely as the only eye
> Of the one-eyed man walking towards the blind.

Time obediently did as he asked. His image is included in the tabernacle of our epoch. But what a gift of prophecy was needed to devine and foreknow it then! Or take another passage:

> Is it for you to understand why,
> Serenely, through storms of mockery,
> I bear my soul upon a dish
> To feed the years to come.

"Let all flesh be still and all men stand in fear and trembling and let no earthly thought be conceived. The King of kings and the Lord of lords comes to lay down his life and to give himself to be the food of the faithful."[28] It is impossible to miss the liturgical parallel.

Unlike the "classical" writers who attached importance to the meaning of prayers and psalms, unlike Pushkin who retold St Ephraim in his "Desert Fathers" and Alexey Tolstoy who paraphrased the requiem prayers of St John Damascene in verse,[29] to Blok, Mayakovsky and Yesenin the textual passages from the prayers and psalms chanted in church were as dear and precious in their literality as were random words of current speech and other fragments of everyday reality picked up at home or in the street.

These quarries of ancient art prompted Mayakovsky to give a parodic structure to his poems. His poetry abounds in analogies with theological concepts, at times implicit, at others stressed. The use of this material called for hugeness, it needed a strong pair of hands and it trained the poet's daring.

It is good that neither Mayakovsky nor Yesenin turned away from what they still remembered having known in childhood – good that they dug this familiar ground, extracted its beauty and made use of it instead of leaving it buried.

When I came to know Mayakovsky better I discovered certain unexpected points of similarity in our technique – in the structure of our images for example, and in our use of rhyme. His poetry delighted me by the beauty and felicity of its movement. I could have asked for nothing better for myself. I wished neither to repeat what he was doing nor to seem to copy him; I repressed instead those tendencies in myself which echoed his – the striving for effects and the heroic tone, which in my case would have been false. This helped me to restrain and purify my style.

As a poet, Mayakovsky was not isolated, he was not a voice crying in a desert; he had neighbours and competitors. Before the revolution Igor Severyanin was his rival on the stage. In the arena of the people's revolution and in people's hearts his rival was Sergey Yesenin.

Severyanin was the king of the concert halls and, in stage

terms, "always sure to fill the house". He warbled his poems to the accompaniment of two or three tunes taken from French operas and managed to be neither vulgar nor offensive to the ear.

His backwardness, his slick verbal innovations and his lack of taste, combined with his enviably pure and fluent poetic diction, created a new and curious genre – a banal version of the delayed impact of the Turgenev cult on poetry.

As for Sergey Yesenin, never since Koltsov had Russia given birth to anything more natural, intrinsic, fitting and generic to her than his talent. Light, free, unburdened by the weight of conscious application which clogged the populists, he was Russia's magnificently lavish gift to us. And with all this, Yesenin was a pulsating lump of that magic artistry, and a living part of that high tradition which, after Pushkin, we should call Mozartian – the Mozartian principle in art, the Mozartian climate.

Yesenin treated his life like a fairytale. Like Prince Ivan, he leapt across the seas mounted on his grey wolf and captured his fire-bird, Isadora Duncan by the tail.[30]

So too, he used magic recipes for making poetry, now playing patience with his words, now writing them with his life's blood. Best of all in him was his vision of his native countryside, the Central-Russian forest country near Ryazan, a vision which he conveyed with overwhelming freshness, as it had come to him in childhood.

Mayakovsky's talent was heavier and rougher than Yesenin's, but perhaps it had more depth and a wider grasp. He was the poet, not of nature like Yesenin, but of the labyrinth of the great modern city in which the lonely spirit of our time, whose passionate, dramatic and inhuman situations he describes, has become confused and lost its way.

As I have said, I had less in common with Mayakovsky than was often thought. One day, when we were arguing at Aseyev's and our disagreement grew particularly sharp, Mayakovsky defined the difference between us with his usual humour: "It's true that we really are different," he told me, "you love lightning in the sky, and I love it in an electric iron."

I could never understand his propagandist zeal, his determination to force himself and his companions on the attention of the public, his campaigning, his industrial team spirit in poetry, or his submission to the voice of actuality.

Still less could I see the point of his paper, *Lef*,[31] of the composition of its board or of its system of ideas. The only honest and consistent member of this group of dissenters was Tretyakov who at least drew logical conclusions from his premises. Like Plato he believed that there could be no room for art in a young socialist state, at any rate at its inception. Certainly the pseudo-art which flourished in the pages of *Lef* – mechanical, uncreative, ruined by editorial corrections made to fit the times – was never worth the care and effort spent on it and could easily have been spared.

From his *Mystery Buffo* onwards and apart from his last and deathless document, *Full Voice*, I could make nothing of Mayakovsky's later poetry. I could make nothing of its clumsy, rhyming dictums, its elaborate triteness, its hackneyed commonplaces or their dull, confused, affected exposition. None of this, to my mind, had anything to do with Mayakovsky – there was no Mayakovsky in it. And yet astonishingly, it is this non-existent Mayakovsky who came to be regarded as revolutionary.

All the same, people continued to think of us, mistakenly, as friends. When, for instance, Yesenin was dissatisfied with imagism and wished to make his peace with Mayakovsky, he chose me as an intermediary (thinking me best fitted for this role) and asked me to arrange a meeting with him.

Although I addressed Mayakovsky as "you" and Yesenin as "thou", I saw even less of Yesenin than of Mayakovsky. I could count my meetings with Yesenin on my fingers, and they always ended in a fantastic scene. Either we swore friendship and shed floods of tears or we fought and people had to drag us apart.

*

In the last years of Mayakovsky's life, when there was no more poetry, neither his own nor anyone else's, when Yesenin hanged himself, when, to put it quite simply, literature ceased to exist (for, after all, the start of *Quiet Flows the Don* was also poetry, as were the early writings of Pilnyak and Babel, Fedin and Vsevolod Ivanov)[32] – in those years, Aseyev, a true friend and a gifted and intelligent man who retained his inward freedom and refused to blind himself to anything, was Mayakovsky's mainstay and his closest friend, nearest to him in mind.

Our ways had parted for good.[33] The reason for our final break was that although I had resigned both as a contributor to *Lef* and as a member of its group, my name continued to be printed on the list of its supporters; I wrote sharply to Mayakovsky and my letter must have made him furious.

Much earlier, while I was still under the spell of his inward strength, enthusiasm and immense claims and possibilities as an artist, and while he returned my liking with equal warmth, I had sent him my book, *My Sister, Life*, with the following lines included in the dedication:

> You are concerned about our balance sheet,
> The tragedy of the S.C.P.E.,[34]
> You who like a Flying Dutchman
> Sang in all the skies of poetry!
> I know, you are sincere,
> But what, along the path
> Of your sincerity, has brought you
> Beneath the vaults of this old people's home?

Two famous dictums were made concerning this period.[35] One was that life was better, life was merrier than in the past; the other that Mayakovsky had been and remained the best and the most gifted poet of our era. I thanked the author of these words in a personal letter because they rescued me from the over-inflation of my significance, to which I had started to become subject in the middle of the Thirties, at the time of the Writers Congress.[36] I love my life and am happy with it. I do not need any extra gilding for it. I cannot conceive of a life that has no secrecy, no privacy, a life lived in the crystalline glitter of a display window.

Mayakovsky began to be introduced forcibly, like potatoes under Catherine the Great. This was his second death. He had no hand in it.

5. THREE SHADOWS

It was in July 1917 that Ehrenburg sought me out on the advice of Bryusov. That was how I came to know this clever writer, a man whose make-up, active and sociable, is the opposite of mine.

This was the beginning of the big influx of Russians who were coming home – former emigrants from the Old Régime, people whom the outbreak of the war had found abroad and who had been interned, and others. Andrey Bely, who had come from Switzerland, and Ehrenburg were among them.

Ehrenburg spoke very highly of Tsvetayeva and showed me her poems.[1] Once at the beginning of the revolution I heard her read her verses at a meeting; she was one of several speakers on the platform. Another time, in winter, during the period of War Communism,[2] I went to see her on some errand; I spoke of trifles and she spoke of trifles in reply. I could make nothing of her work.

At that time, my ear was vitiated by our verbal whirligigs and the twisting and chopping of all familiar things which was going on everywhere. Anything said in a normal way bounced off me. I forgot that words could have a sense and content of their own, without the tinkling ornaments we hung on them.

The very harmony of Tsvetayeva's poems, their clear meaning, the fact that they had only merits and there was nothing wrong with them, were to me an obstacle and prevented me from seeing their essence. I wasn't looking for the essence of things, only for their incidental sharpness.

I continued to underrate Tsvetayeva for a long time, just

as in different ways I underrated many others – Bagritsky, Khlebnikov, Mandelstamm, Gumilyov.

I have already said that while the rest of us were unable to give an intelligible account of ourselves and made a virtue of inarticulacy and a necessity of originality, only two, Aseyev and Tsvetayeva, could express themselves properly and write in a classical language and style.

There came a day when both of them gave up their skill: Aseyev was seduced by Khlebnikov's example and Tsvetayeva went through an inner transformation of her own. But by then I had fallen under the charm of the earlier, traditional, unregenerate Tsvetayeva.

You had to read your way into her. When I had done this, I was amazed by her boundless strength and purity. There was nothing like it anywhere else. To put it briefly – I can honestly say that if you except Annensky, Blok and with certain reservations Bely, Tsvetayeva's early manner was exactly what all the symbolists, from first to last, dreamed of and did not achieve. And while they spluttered helplessly in their linguistic ocean of lifeless schemes and dead archaic forms, Tsvetayeva soared over the real difficulties of creation, solving its problem effortlessly and with matchless technical brilliance.

It was not until the spring of 1922, after she had left Russia, that I came across her booklet, *Versty*, in a Moscow book-shop. I was immediately overcome by the immense lyrical power of her poetic form. It was a form which had sprung living from experience – personal, and neither narrow-chested nor short of breath from line to line but rich and compact and enveloping whole sequences of stanza after stanza in its vast periods of unbroken rhythm.

I felt a kinship with something which lay beyond these individual qualities – an experience, perhaps, of the same influences, or of common factors in the formation of character, such as the role of home and music in my life, a similarity of points of departure, tastes and aspirations.

Tsvetayeva was in Prague. I sent her an enthusiastic letter, full of my astonishment at failing to appreciate her for so long and at discovering her so late. She replied, and we went on exchanging letters. Our correspondence became more frequent in the middle Twenties, when her *Craft* was published, and when her *End Poem, Hill Poem* and *Ratcatcher* – all vast in scope and meaning, vivid and magnificently new – were seen in manuscript in Moscow. That was how we became friends.

In the summer of 1935,[3] when I was on the verge of mental illness after almost twelve months of insomnia, I found myself at an anti-Fascist congress in Paris. There I met Tsvetayeva's son and daughter and her husband, an enchanting, sensitive and steadfast being of whom I grew as fond as of a brother.

Tsvetayeva's family were pressing her to return to Russia. It was partly that they were homesick, partly that they sympathised with Communism and the Soviet Union; and partly that they thought Tsvetayeva had no sort of life in Paris and was going to pieces in loneliness and isolation from her readers.

She asked me what I thought about it. I had no definite opinion. It was hard to know what to advise them; I was afraid that these remarkable people would have a difficult and troubled time at home. But the tragedy which was to strike the whole family surpassed my fears beyond all measure.

When I was speaking of my childhood at the beginning of this sketch, I described actual events and scenes, but further on I confined myself to generalities and brief impressions. I had to do this for lack of space.

If I were to tell the story of my friendship with Tsvetayeva incident by incident and step by step, including all the interests and hopes which brought us together, I would soon outrun the limits I have set myself. It would need a whole book, so much did we experience together – so many changes, joys and tragedies, always unexpected and always widening our horizons.

But here, as in what remains to be said, I will keep away from personal and private things and mention only what is general and essential.

Tsvetayeva was a woman with an actively male soul, decisive, militant and indomitable. In her life and works she rushed headlong, hungrily and almost rapaciously, into the search for finality and definition, in the pursuit of which she had ventured far afield and outstripped everyone else.

Apart from her few known works she wrote many others which are unknown in Russia, huge, stormy compositions, some in the style of Russian folk-lore, others on general historic, mythological and legendary themes.

Their publication will be a triumph and a revelation for our native poetry which, in a single moment, will be enriched by all these overdue gifts.

I believe that the re-evaluation and the recognition which await Tsvetayeva will be very great.

We were friends. I had almost a hundred of her letters, written in reply to mine. For all that I have said of the importance in my life of things vanished or lost, I could never have imagined that I would lose these priceless and treasured letters. I lost them through excessive care to keep them safe.

During the war, when I used to visit my family in the country to which they had been evacuated, a member of the staff of the Scriabin Museum, who was a great friend of mine and a great admirer of Tsvetayeva, offered to look after them together with some letters from my parents and a few from Gorky and Romain Rolland. She put them in the safe of the Museum – all except Tsvetayeva's; these she kept by her, never letting them out of her sight and not even trusting them to the fireproof safe.

She lived all the year round in the country and took the letters with her every day, in a small attaché-case, to and from her work. One winter's evening she was going home utterly exhausted. When she was half-way home from the country station, walking through the wood, she realised that she had left the case in the coach of the suburban train. That was how Tsvetayeva's letters were borne away and vanished.

Over the decades since the publication of *Safe Conduct*, I have several times thought that if it were to be reissued, I would add a chapter about the Caucasus and the two Georgian poets. But time has gone by and there has seemed no need for other additions. The only lacuna has been this missing chapter. Now I will write this account.

It was in winter, in about 1930, that the poet Paolo Yashvili and his wife came to see me in Moscow. He was brilliant, polished, cultured, an amusing talker, European and good-looking.

Soon after this, there were painful upheavals, changes and complications which involved two families, my own and that of my closest friends. For a long time neither I nor my companion, who was later to become my second wife,[4] had anywhere to lay our heads. Yashvili offered us a refuge in his house in Tiflis.[5]

In those days I knew nothing about the Caucasus or Georgia, nothing about the Georgians or their life. It was all a complete revelation to me. Everything was unfamiliar and everything was astonishing. The huge dark stormy mountains looming at the end of every street in Tiflis. The home life of the poor carried on out of doors, bolder, less in hiding, more frank and vivid than in the north. The symbolism of folk traditions, full of mysticism and messianism, giving imagination its cue, and making a poet out of everyone, as in Catholic Poland.[6] The high level of culture of the leading section of society – an active intellectual life which, by then, was rarely to be found elsewhere. The better districts of the town, their cosy nooks, recalling Petersburg, their first-floor window bars bent into the shapes of lyres and flower-baskets; the picturesque back streets. The beat of tambourines, drumming the Lezginka, perpetually at your heels and overtaking you at every turn. The goat-like bleating of bagpipes and the sound of other instruments. The advent of the evening in a southern town, full of stars, and of the smells of gardens, pastry-shops and coffee-houses.

Yashvili was a remarkable poet of the post-symbolist period. His verse is built on the precise and carefully established evidence of the senses. It has affinities with the modern European prose of Bely, Hamsun, Proust, and, like their prose, it has the freshness of sharp and unexpected observations. It is supremely creative, not cluttered up with tightly packed effects, but airy, spacious, full of breath and movements.

The outbreak of the First World War found Yashvili in Paris where he was studying at the Sorbonne. He set out for home by a roundabout way. At a small station in Norway he gaped and missed his train. A young Norwegian and his wife, who had come by sleigh from some remote farm to fetch the mail, noticed the predicament of the fiery southerner and took pity on him. They managed somehow to communicate with him and carried him off to their farm to wait for the next train which was not due until the following day.

Yashvili told stories wonderfully. He was a born teller of adventure tales. He was always getting into unexpected situations, and they always had the style of a well written short story. Chance happenings positively sought him out and clung to him; he had a lucky hand with them, it was his special gift.

Talent radiated from him. His eyes shone with an inner fire; the fire of passion had scorched his lips and the heat of experience had burnt and blackened his face, so that he looked older than his years and as though he had been worn and tattered by life.

On the day we arrived he gathered his friends, members of a group of which he was the leader. I don't remember who was there that time. Probably his next-door neighbour, Nikolay Nadiradze, a genuine and first-rate lyric poet. And Titsian Tabidze and his wife.

*

I remember that room as if it were today. How indeed could I forget it? Carefully, not to shatter its image – before I knew what terrors were reserved for it – I let it sink that very evening to the bottom of my soul, with all the frightening things that later were to happen in it and around it.

Why were these two people sent to me? How can one describe our relations? They both became an integral part of my private world. I did not prefer one to the other, they were so inseparable, they so complemented one another.

The fate of both of them, together with the fate of Tsvetayeva, was to become my greatest cause for grief.

If the expression of Yashvili's personality was outward-looking, centrifugal, Tabidze was withdrawn into himself, and his every line and his every gesture were an invitation into the interior of his soul, rich in intuition and presentiment.

The astonishing thing about his poetry was the feeling it conveyed of unexhausted lyrical reserves, the feeling that the unspoken and what remained for him to say outweighed everything he had already said. The presence of these still untouched resources of the spirit was the background of his verse, it gave it added depth and that specific mood which held it and which is its great and bitter charm. There is as much soul in his poetry as there was in him, a reserved and complicated soul, wholly attracted to the good and capable of clairvoyance and self-sacrifice.

Thinking of Yashvili I think of urban situations – rooms, arguments, public meetings, Yashvili sparkling with eloquence at crowded parties at night.

The memory of Tabidze puts me in mind of the country; landscapes rise in my imagination, the waves of the sea and a vast flowering plain; clouds drifting in a row and, behind them in the distance, mountains rising to the same level. Merging into this background is the stocky, thick-set figure of the smiling poet. He has a jerky step and when he laughs his whole body shakes. Now he rises, turns sideways to the table and knocks his knife against a tumbler calling for silence – he is about to make a speech. His habit of raising one shoulder higher than the other gives him a lop-sided look.

The house in Kodzhory[7] stands on the corner of the main street at the bend. The road climbs past its façade, curves around it and carries on past its rear wall. All passers-by on foot or otherwise, can be seen from the building twice.

This was at the time when, according to Bely, the triumph of materialism had done away with all material things. There was nothing to eat or to put on. There was nothing tangible, nothing existed except ideas. If we kept alive, it was thanks to our Caucasian friends who performed miracles for our benefit, getting and bringing us what we needed most, and raising loans for us from publishers against our non-existent assets....

We are all gathered together, we share our news, have supper and read aloud to one another. A small, fresh wind quickly runs its fingers over the silver poplar leaves, turning them over and showing their white velvet linings. The air is full of dazing southern fragrance as of rumours. And high up, like any cart turning on its axle, the night slowly turns its lumbering wagon of stars. And people, cars and carts move along the road, and everyone is seen from the house twice.

Or we are on the Georgian Military Highway, or at Borzhóm or at Abastumán. Or, after journeys, sights, adventures, drinking, we are at Bakuryány (I, for my part, with a black eye from having fallen flat on my face) at the house of Leonidze, the most original of all poets, the one closest to the secrets of his language and therefore least translatable.

We picnic in the woods at night; Leonidze has a beautiful wife and two small, enchanting daughters. And next day a *mestvire* – a wandering minstrel – comes with his bagpipes and improvises a poem in honour of each guest as we all sit round the table, seizing on every pretext for a toast – even my black eye will serve.

Or we are staying by the sea at Kobulety; it rains and storms, and in the same hotel with us is young Simon Chikovani, the future master of a brilliant visual poetic style. We walk together, and always beside me, and above the line of mountains and horizons, I see the smiling poet's head, and the bright signs of his outstanding gifts and the shadow of sadness and destiny on his smile and face. And as I take my leave of him in these pages once again, now let me, in his person, take leave of all my other memories.

6. CONCLUSION

Here I end my sketch. I am not cutting it short or leaving it unfinished. I am ending it exactly where I meant to end it from the very first. I had no intention of writing the history of half a century in many volumes and with many characters.

There are many good poets whom I have not included in my sketch – Martynov, Zabolotsky, Selvinsky, Tikhonov – all good poets. I have not said anything about the poets of the generation of Simonov and Tvardovsky, which counts so many of them.

I have deliberately kept within the narrowest circle of my life, limiting myself to this.

What I have written is enough to give some idea of how, in my individual case, life became converted into art and art was born of life and of experience.

I have already said how divided is my attitude to my poetic past – my own and that of many others. I would not lift a finger to rescue more than a quarter of my writings from oblivion. Why then have I agreed to have a collection of my poems published?[1]

There are two reasons. One is that, for all that spoils them and that saddens and annoys me in them, they do contain some particles of what they should contain – a few exact and successful discoveries.

The other is that quite recently I have completed my main and most important work, the only one of which I am not ashamed and for which I answer without a qualm – a novel in prose with additions in verse, *Doctor Zhivago*. The poems assembled in this book, which are scattered across all the years of my life, constitute preparatory stages to the novel. Indeed, I view their republication as a preparation for the novel.

Here ends my biographical sketch. To take it further would be immeasurably difficult. If I went on with it, keeping to the sequence of events, I would have to speak of years and circumstances, of people and of destinies contained within the framework of the revolution. Of a world of aims and aspirations, problems and achievements previously unknown, and of a new restraint, a new severity and new trials which it imposed on human personality, pride, honour, industry and endurance.

This world, unique and not to be compared with any other, has now withdrawn into the distance of memory; it looms on the horizon like mountains seen from a plain, or like a distant city smoking in its night glow.

To write of it one should write in such a way as to make the hair rise and the heart falter. To write of it by rote and habit, to write less than overwhelmingly, to write less vividly than Gogol or Dostoyevsky wrote of Petersburg, would be not only without sense or purpose – it would be base and shameless.

We are still far from this ideal way of writing.

POEMS 1955–1959

Во всем мне хочется дойти
До самой сути:
В работе, в поисках пути,
В сердечной смуте.

До сущности протекших дней,
До их причины,
До оснований, до корней,
До сердцевины.

Все время схватывая нить
Судеб, событий,
Жить, думать, чувствовать, любить,
Свершать открытья.

О, если бы я только мог,
Хотя отчасти,
Я написал бы восемь строк
О свойствах страсти!

О беззаконьях, о грехах,
Бегах, погонях,
Нечаянностях впопыхах,
Локтях, ладонях.

Я вывел бы ее закон,
Ее начало,
И повторял ее имен
Инициалы.

Я б разбивал стихи как сад.
Всей дрожью жилок
Цвели бы липы в них подряд —
Гуськом, в затылок.

I want the heart of the matter
Always, in work,
The chaos of feelings,
The quest for a way;

The meaning, cause,
Foundations, roots
And kernel
Of vanished days;

As I trace the links
Between lives and events,
Explore,
Live, think, feel, love.

If I could muster
However crude
A dozen lines
On the properties of passion,

Its vandalism,
Pursuits and panics,
Impromptus,
Hustling and hands;

Deducing its principles,
Repeating aloud
The initials of its names,
I'd lay out my stanzas

Like landscape gardens;
A shiver of sap
And my lines would bloom
Into rows of lime trees.

В стихи б я внес дыханье роз,
Дыханье мяты,
Луга, осоку, сенокос,
Грозы раскаты.

Так некогда Шопен вложил
Живое чудо
Фольварков, парков, рощ, могил
В свои этюды.

Достигнутого торжества
Игра и мука —
Натянутая тетива
Тугого лука.

I'd air my stanzas
With mint and roses,
With haymaking, rushes
And rolling storms,

Like Chopin, who conjured
Alive his studies
With woods, parks, tombs
And country houses.

The fun and the torment
Of such a triumph
Bend the bow
And tense the string.

Быть знаменитым — некрасиво.
Не это подымает ввысь.
Не надо заводить архива,
Над рукописями трястись.

Цель творчества — самоотдача,
А не шумиха, не успех.
Позорно, ничего не знача,
Быть притчей на устах у всех.

Но надо жить без самозванства,
Так жить, чтобы в конце концов
Привлечь к себе любовь пространства,
Услышать будущего зов.

И надо оставлять пробелы
В судьбе, а не среди бумаг,
Места и главы жизни целой
Отчеркивая на полях.

И окунаться в неизвестность
И прятать в ней свои шаги,
Как прячется в тумане местность,
Когда в нем не видать ни зги.

Другие по живому следу
Пройдут твой путь за пядью пядь,
Но пораженья от победы
Ты сам не должен отличать.

И должен ни единой долькой
Не отступаться от лица,
Но быть живым, живым и только,
Живым и только до конца.

Fame's not a pretty sight,
Won't lift you to the clouds.
No need to hoard your notes
Or tremble over what you write.

Success is not your aim,
Nor noise, but gift of self.
Shameful to be a legend
On all lips, and an empty name.

To win, before you die,
The friendship of the spaces
And hear the future speak
Means living a life and not a lie.

Censor what the world reads
Not of your books, but you;
A sideline in the margin
Is all a chapter of living needs.

Merge into privacy
Like landscape into fog,
Blinding the passer-by
With absolute nothingness to see.

Though other pairs of feet
Will tread your living footsteps
It's not for you to settle
What's victory and what's defeat.

And yet you must defend
Each inch of your position,
To be alive, only
Alive, only alive to the end.

ДУША

Душа моя, печальница
О всех в кругу моем,
Ты стала усыпальницей
Замученных живьем.

Тела их бальзамируя,
Им посвящая стих,
Рыдающею лирою
Оплакивая их.

Ты в наше время шкурное
За совесть и за страх
Стоишь могильной урною,
Покоящей их прах.

Их муки совокупные
Тебя склонили ниц.
Ты пахнешь пылью трупною
Мертвецких и гробниц.

Душа моя, скудельница,
Все, виденное здесь,
Перемолов, как мельница,
Ты превратила в смесь.

И дальше перемалывай
Все бывшее со мной,
Как сорок лет без малого,
В погостный перегной.

SOUL

Soul in mourning
For agonised lives,
You are the vault
That buried my friends,

Embalming their bodies
In dedicated verse;
Harp of bitterness
Of my bereavement;

Funeral urn
That stands like conscience
In a skinflint time,
Giving rest to their ashes.

Their weight of agony
Has bent you down;
You smell like a morgue
With the dust of the dead.

My soul, mass grave
Grinding an age
To a heap of compost,
These forty years

I fed you the grist
Of my own experience;
Grind what I witnessed
To graveyard dung.

ЕВА

Стоят деревья у воды,
И полдень с берега крутого
Закинул облака в пруды,
Как переметы рыболова.

Как невод, тонет небосвод,
И в это небо, точно в сети
Толпа купальщиков плывет,
Мужчины, женщины и дети.

Пять-шесть купальщиц в лозняке
Выходят на берег без шума
И выжимают на песке
Свои купальные костюмы.

И, на подобие ужей,
Ползут и вьются кольца пряжи,
Как будто искуситель-змей
Скрывался в мокром трикотаже.

О, женщина, твой вид и взгляд
Ничуть меня в тупик не ставят.
Ты вся, как горла перехват,
Когда его волненье сдавит.

Ты создана как бы вчерне,
Как строчка из другого цикла,
Как будто не шутя во сне
Из моего ребра возникла.

И тотчас вырвалась из рук
И выскользнула из объятья,
Сама смятенье и испуг
И сердца мужеского сжатье.

EVE

Trees line the water. The day
Stands on a neighbouring hill
Casting into the lake
Its nets of cloud; clouds fill

With shoals of bathers, man
And woman, woman and child
Pell-mell, a heavy haul
For this summer fisherman.

Now half a dozen girls
Noiselessly come to land,
Emerge from reeds, wring out
Their costumes on the sand;

The water-logged material
Wriggles as if the weave
Was woven with a snake,
The snake that tempted Eve.

Eve, you can't flummox me
By giving me the eye;
I know you, noose of tenseness
Squeezing my gullet dry.

You're a rough draft, a line
Of a different cycle of verse;
Perhaps I dreamed you up
Out of a rib of mine,

But when I hugged you back
You wrenched yourself apart
Frightened, to frighten men
Like a seizure of the heart.

БЕЗ НАЗВАНИЯ

Недотрога, тихоня в быту,
Ты сейчас вся огонь, вся — горенье.
Дай, запру я твою красоту
В темном тереме стихотворенья.

Посмотри, как преображена
Огневой кожурой абажура
Конура, край стены, край окна,
Наши тени и наши фигуры.

Ты с ногами сидишь на тахте,
Под себя их поджав по-турецки.
Все равно, на свету, в темноте —
Ты всегда рассуждаешь по-детски.

За беседой ты нижешь на шнур
Горсть на платье скатившихся бусин.
Слишком грустен твой вид, чересчур
Разговор твой прямой безыскусен.

Пошло слово «любовь», ты права;
Я придумаю кличку иную.
Для тебя я весь мир, все слова,
Если хочешь, переименую.

Разве хмурый твой вид передаст
Чувств твоих рудоносную залежь,
Сердца тайно светящийся пласт?
Для чего же глаза ты печалишь?

NO TITLE

Miss touch-me-not's on fire,
The prude of every day.
In the dark turret of a poem
I'll lock your looks away.

The lampshade's fiery skin
Transforms the room, makes free
With cramped walls, window sill,
Our shadows, you and me.

You tuck your feet beneath you
Like a Turk, on the divan,
Reason (you always do)
As only children can,

Daydream, threading the beads
That spilt across your dress,
Look much too sad and chatter
With too much artlessness.

You're right, I must rename love;
It's a word we have all worn through.
If you like, I'll christen the world
And all its words, for you.

But how can dark looks show me
What ore of feeling lies
At the hidden mine of your heart?
Why do you cloud your eyes?

ПЕРЕМЕНА

Я льнул когда-то к беднякам —
Не из возвышенного взгляда,
А потому, что только там
Шла жизнь без помпы и парада.

Хотя я с барством был знаком
И с публикою деликатной,
Я дармоедству был врагом
И другом голи перекатной.

И я старался дружбу свесть
С людьми из трудового званья,
За что и делали мне честь,
Меня считая тоже рванью.

Был осязателен без фраз,
Вещественен, телесен, весок
Уклад подвалов без прикрас
И чердаков без занавесок.

И я испортился с тех пор,
Как времени коснулась порча,
И горе возвели в позор,
Мещан и оптимистов корча.

Всем тем, кому я доверял,
Я с давних пор уже неверен.
Я человека потерял,
С тех пор, как всеми он потерян.

CHANGE

Not from high-mindedness,
But wanting something more
Than pomp, puff and parade,
I lived among the poor;

Well knowing cream of culture
And social paragon,
Preferred the down-and-outs
Before the hangers-on

And looked for friends who followed
The labourer's vocation,
Honoured when asked to join
Their rag-bag congregation.

Weighty, with no fine phrases
To prove that they were there,
Stood naked basements, attics
Without a blind to wear.

But while the optimists
Turned grief to shame, with sneers,
I caught the epidemic
Corruption of these years.

Traitor to all I trusted
Since many years ago
I end by losing man
Like all the men I know.

ВЕСНА В ЛЕСУ

Отчаянные холода
Задерживали таянье.
Весна позднее, чем всегда,
Но и зато нечаянней.

С утра амурится петух,
И нет прохода курице.
Сосна, оборотясь на юг,
Лицом на солнце жмурится.

Хотя и парит и печет,
Еще недели целые
Дороги сковывает лед
Корою почернелою.

В лесу еловый мусор, хлам,
И снегом все завалено.
Водою с солнцем пополам
Затоплены проталины.

И небо в тучах, как в пуху,
Над грязной вешней жижицей
Застряло в сучьях наверху
И от жары не движется.

SPRING IN THE FOREST

Desperate cold
Fought back the thaw.
Spring's late
And all the more startling.

Cock pesters hen
With daylong gallantry.
Blinking, the pine
Turns south in the sunlight.

For steaming and baking
Weeks on end
Black ice
Chains up the roads.

Pines dump their rubbish
In snow-stacked woods;
The slush cascades
Into sun and water.

Bolstered with downy
Clouds, the sky
Sticks in the branches,
Helpless with heat.

ИЮЛЬ

По дому бродит привиденье.
Весь день шаги над головой.
На чердаке мелькают тени.
По дому бродит домовой.

Везде болтается некстати,
Мешается во все дела,
В халате крадется к кровати,
Срывает скатерть со стола.

Ног у порога не обтерши,
Вбегает в вихре сквозняка
И с занавеской, как с танцоршей,
Взвивается до потолка.

Кто этот баловник-невежа
И этот пркзрак и двойник?
Да это наш жилец приезжий,
Наш летний дачник-отпускник.

На весь его недолгий роздых
Мы целый дом ему сдаем.
Июль с грозой, июльский воздух
Снял комнаты у нас внаем.

Июль, таскающий в одеже
Пух одуванчиков, лопух.
Июль, домой сквозь окна вхожий,
Все громко говорящий вслух.

Степной нечесанный растрепа,
Пропахший липой и травой,
Ботвой и запахом укропа,
Июльский воздух луговой.

JULY

All day, steps overhead.
The attic flickers with shadows.
The rooms are haunted
By the genius of the house,

A busybody
Who jerks the table-cloth,
Borrows your dressing-gown,
Steals to your bed,

Whirls in with draughts
And unwiped feet,
Waltzes the curtain
Up to the ceiling.

Who's this buffoon,
Ghost and guest,
On leave
In our country house?

We rent him our rooms
For his short-lived holiday,
The storming
Air of July;

Whose clothes are tweedy
With burrs and dandelions,
Chatterbox
Bouncing through windows,

Smelling of grass,
Lime, beet-leaves, fennel;
Shock-headed tramp
From the back of beyond.

ПО ГРИБЫ

Плетемся по грибы.
Шоссе. Леса. Канавы.
Дорожные столбы
Налево и направо.

С широкого шоссе
Идем во тьму лесную.
По щиколку в росе
Плутаем врассыпную.

А солнце под кусты
На грузди и волнушки
Чрез дебри темноты
Бросает свет с опушки.

Гриб прячется за пень.
На пень садится птица.
Нам вехой служит тень,
Чтобы с пути не сбиться.

Но время в сентябре
Отмерено так куцо,
Едва ль до нас заре
Сквозь чащу дотянуться.

Набиты кузовки,
Наполнены корзины,
Одни боровики
У доброй половины.

Уходим. За спиной
Стеною лес недвижный,
Где день в красе земной
Сгорел скоропостижно.

PICKING MUSHROOMS

Road and milestones.
Trees and ditches.
We shuffle away
To look for mushrooms,

One by one
Dive out of daylight
To paddle
In soaking forest.

The sun, from a clearing
In thickets of darkness,
Gropes under bushes
For brown and yellow mushrooms

That lurk by a tree-stump,
A bench for a bird.
We've only our shadows
For signposts.

September rations
The hours so brief,
The twilight fumbles
And fails to find us.

Home with our baskets
Stuffed to bursting,
Pine-mushrooms
Half the haul.

Behind us the day,
Stonewalled by the forest,
Burns swiftly down
In worldly splendour.

ТИШИНА

Пронизан солнцем лес насквозь.
Лучи стоят столбами пыли.
Отсюда, уверяют, лось
Выходит на дорог развилье.

В лесу молчанье, тишина,
Как будто жизнь в глухой лощине
Не солнцем заворожена,
А по совсем другой причине.

Действительно, невдалеке
Средь заросли стоит лосиха.
Пред ней деревья в столбняке.
Вот отчего в лесу так тихо.

Лосиха ест лесной подсед,
Хрустя, обгладывает молодь.
Задевши за ее хребет,
Болтается на ветке жолудь.

Иван-да-Марья, зверобой,
Ромашка, Иван-чай, татарник,
Опутанные ворожбой,
Глазеют, обступив кустарник.

Во всем лесу один ручей
В овраге, полном благозвучья,
Твердит то тише, то звончей
Про этот небывалый случай.

Звеня на всю лесную падь
И оглашая лесосеку
Он что-то хочет рассказать
Почти словами человека.

STILLNESS

Pillars of dusty sunlight
Build arcades through the forest.
    The road forks; here,
Says rumour, the deer break cover.

The quiet insists. A clearing
Waits in the distance, awestruck
    Not by the sun;
Look for a different reason

Lost in the bushes: a doe
That silences the forest
    For trees become
As dumb as posts before her.

She nibbles a lunch of sapling;
The green wood crunches; an acorn
    Catching her spine
Swings on the tail of a twig.

Cow-wheat and camomile,
St. John's wort, cotton-thistle
    Stand round and stare,
Can't tear themselves away.

Now muted, ringing now,
A stream in a sounding hollow
    Tells the whole forest
The unprecedented news;

Reaches the forester
With babble, brimming over
    To speak to him
In almost human words.

СТОГА

Снуют пунцовые стрекозы,
Летят шмели во все концы.
Колхозницы смеются с возу,
Проходят с косами косцы.

Пока хорошая погода,
Гребут и ворошат корма
И складывают до захода
В стога, величиной с дома.

Стог принимает на закате
Вид постоялого двора,
Где ночь ложится на полати
В накошенные клевера.

К утру, когда потемки реже,
Стог высится, как сеновал,
В котором месяц мимоезжий,
Зарывшись, переночевал.

Чем свет — телега за телегой
Лугами катятся впотьмах.
Наставший день встает с ночлега
С трухой и сеном в волосах.

А в полдень вновь синеют выси.
Опять стога, как облака,
Опять, как водка на анисе,
Земля душиста и крепка.

HAYSTACKS

Red flashes of dragonflies,
Laughter of women from waggons,
Bumble of bees, and reapers
  Humping their scythes.

While the weather holds they rake
And turn the hay, stack it
  Before night falls
In ricks as tall as houses.

Against the setting sun
The rick sets up as an inn
  Where night gets ready
To go to bed on clover.

Dark softens towards the dawn;
The rick looms like a loft
  Where a wayfaring moon
Digs in to sleep till day.

At first light cart after cart
Rolls darkly through the fields.
The day gets out of bed
  With hay in its hair.

And at noon the ricks are clouds,
The sky is blue, the earth
  Has body and strength
Like vodka with aniseed.

ЛИПОВАЯ АЛЛЕЯ

Ворота с полукруглой аркой.
Холмы, луга, леса, овсы.
В ограде мрак и холод парка
И дом невиданной красы.

Там липы в несколько обхватов
Справляют в сумраке аллей,
Вершины друг за друга спрятав,
Свой двухсотлетний юбилей.

Они смыкают сверху своды.
Внизу — лужайка и цветник,
Который правильные ходы
Пересекают напрямик.

Под липами, как в подземельи,
Ни светлой точки на песке,
И лишь отверстием туннеля
Светлеет выход вдалеке.

Но вот приходят дни цветенья,
И липы в поясе оград
Разбрасывают вместе с тенью
Неотразимый аромат.

Гуляющие в летних шляпах
Вдыхают, кто бы ни прошел,
Непостижимый этот запах,
Доступный пониманью пчел.

Он составляет в эти миги,
Когда он за сердце берет,
Предмет и содержанье книги,
А парк и клумбы — переплет.

AVENUE OF LIMES

Arched gates, hills, fields,
Woods, wheat. Walled darkness
And cold of a park.
A splendid house.

Unembraceably broad
The limes are keeping
In dusky avenues
Their bicentenary.

Putting their heads together
They close the vault
Above lawn and flower bed,
Neat sunless paths,

Leaving no chink
In this underworld
But the exit, further
Than mouth of tunnel.

The days flower, the limes
In their belt of fences
Squander shadow
And a power of scent

Incomprehensible to walkers
In summer hats
But plain
To the clever bees.

Clutching the heart
It makes the matter
Of a book whose binding
Is park and flower beds.

На старом дереве громоздком,
Завешивая сверху дом,
Горят, закапанные воском,
Цветы, зажженные огнем.

A heavy old tree
Curtains the house
With a waxy spatter
Of lighted flowers.

КОГДА РАЗГУЛЯЕТСЯ

Большое озеро как блюдо.
За ним — скопленье облаков,
Нагроможденных белой грудой
Суровых горных ледников.

По мере смены освещенья
И лес меняет колорит.
То весь горит, то черной тенью
Насевшей копоти покрыт.

Когда в исходе дней дождливых
Меж туч проглянет синева,
Как небо празднично в прорывах,
Как торжества полна трава!

Стихает ветер, даль расчистив.
Разлито солнце по земле.
Просвечивает зелень листьев,
Как живопись в цветном стекле.

В церковной росписи оконниц
Так в вечность смотрят изнутри
В мерцающих венцах бессонниц
Святые, схимники, цари.

Как будто внутренность собора
Простор земли, и чрез окно
Далекий отголосок хора
Мне слышать иногда дано.

Природа, мир, тайник вселенной,
Я службу долгую твою,
Объятый дрожью сокровенной,
В слезах от счастья отстою.

WHEN THE WEATHER CLEARS

A massive dish of lake.
Beyond it, a heap of clouds
As grim and white as a heap
    Of mountain glaciers.

With changes in the lighting
The forest changes colour,
On fire, sooty with shadow,
    On fire again.

The passing of the rains
Leaves blue and festive sky
    In tattered cloud
Over jubilees of grass.

The wind cleans up the distance,
Dies down; sun spills on earth
Illuminating leaves
    Like stained glass windows

Where hermits, saints and tsars
Peer, under glinting crowns
    Of sleeplessness,
From church to eternity.

Remote in this far-reaching
Cathedral of the world,
    A choir allows me
The echo of a note.

World's tabernacle, nature,
I kneel[1] through your long service.
    A trembling hugs me;
I cry with happiness.

ХЛЕБ

Ты выводы копишь полвека,
Но их не заносишь в тетрадь,
И если ты сам не калека,
То должен был что-то понять.

Ты понял блаженство занятий,
Удачи закон и секрет.
Ты понял, что праздность — проклятье,
И счастья без подвига нет.

Что ждет алтарей, откровений,
Героев и богатырей
Дремучее царство растений,
Могучее царство зверей.

Что первым таким откровеньем
Остался в сцепленьи судеб
Прапращуром в дар поколеньям
Взрощенный столетьями хлеб.

Что поле во ржи и пшенице
Не только зовет к молотьбе,
Но некогда эту страницу
Твой предок вписал о тебе.

Что это и есть его слово,
Его небывалый почин
Средь круговращенья земного,
Рождений, скорбей и кончин.

BREAD

With half a century to pile,
    Unwritten, your conclusions,
    By now, if you're not a halfwit,
You should have lost a few illusions,

    Grasped the pleasure of study,
The laws and secrets of success,
The curse of idleness, the heroism
    Needed for happiness;

    That the powerful kingdom of beasts,
The sleepy kingdom of vegetation
    Await their heroes, giants,
Their altars and their revelation;

That first of all the revelations,
    Father of living and dead,
Gift to the generations, growth
    Of the centuries, is bread;

And a harvest field is not just wheat
    But a page to understand,
    Written about yourself
In your remote forefather's hand,

His very word, his own amazing
Initiative among the birth,
    Sorrow and death that circle
    Their set ways round the earth.

ОСЕННИЙ ЛЕС

Осенний лес заволосател.
В нем тень и сон и тишина.
Ни белка, ни сова, ни дятел
Его не будят ото сна.

И солнце по тропам осенним
В него входя на склоне дня,
Кругом косится с опасеньем,
Не скрыта ли в нем западня.

В нем топи, кочки и осины
И мхи и заросли ольхи,
И где-то за лесной трясиной
Поют в селенье петухи.

Петух свой окрик прогорланит,
И вот он вновь надолго смолк,
Как будто он раздумьем занят,
Какой в запевке этой толк.

Но где-то в дальнем закоулке
Прокукарекает сосед;
Как часовой из караулки
Петух откликнется в ответ.

Он отзовется словно эхо,
И вот, за петухом петух
Отметят глоткою, как вехой,
Восток и запад, север, юг.

По петушиной перекличке
Расступится к опушке лес
И вновь увидит с непривычки
Поля и даль и синь небес.

AUTUMN FOREST

A forest of shadows
Grows hairy with autumn,
Wakes to no squirrel,
Owl or woodpecker.

The sun slopes in
By autumn paths
At decline of day,
Looking warily round

For a trap in the moss, mounds,
Alders and aspens.
Beyond the marshes
A village cock

Crows raucous,
And keeps a long silence,
Puzzling what sense
There was to his tune.

Cock-a-doodle-doo
From a distant neighbour,
Challenged as prompt
As soldier from sentry-box;

Cock echoes cock
Till a signpost of crowing
Points north, south,
East and west

And the ranks of trees
Step open; the forest
Sees strange new sights:
Blue sky, fields, distance.

ЗАМОРОЗКИ

Холодным утром солнце в дымке
Стоит столбом огня в дыму.
Я тоже, как на скверном снимке,
Совсем неотличим ему.

Пока оно из мглы не выйдет,
Блеснув за прудом на лугу,
Меня деревья плохо видят
На отдаленном берегу.

Прохожий узнается позже,
Чем он пройдет, нырнув в туман.
Мороз покрыт гусиной кожей,
И воздух лжив, как слой румян.

Идешь по инею дорожки,
Как по настилу из рогож.
Земле дышать ботвой картошки
И стынуть — больше невтерпеж.

FIRST FROST

Pillar of fire in smoke, the sun
   In the haze of a frosty morning
      Sees me muzzy
      As a bad photo;

Blazes a trail through pond and meadow
   Enabling puzzled trees
      To pick me out
      Across the water.

Identified too late, a body
   Drowns in the mist. The frost
      Has goose-flesh, smarmy
      With air like rouge.

Sacking of hoarfrost wads the paths.
   The earth is sick and tired
      Of cold and the stink
      Of potato stalks.

НОЧНОЙ ВЕТЕР

Стихли песни и пьяный галдеж.
Завтра надо вставать спозаранок.
В избах гаснут огни. Молодежь
Разошлась по домам с погулянок.

Только ветер бредет наугад
Все по той же заросшей тропинке,
По которой с толпою ребят
Во-свояси он шел с вечеринки.

Он за дверью поник головой.
Он не любит ночных катавасий.
Он бы кончить хотел мировой
В споре с ночью свои несогласья.

Перед ними — заборы садов.
Оба спорят, не могут уняться.
За разборами их неладов
На дороге деревья толпятся.

NIGHT WIND

The village blacks out. The young
Go home from going gay.
The songs and the drunks are silent.
Tomorrow's an early day.

Only the night wind fumbles
A path bewildered among
The weeds, that brought it home
With the party-going young.

It hangs its head at the door,
No stomach for a fight,
Wondering how to settle
Its argument with night.

Between the garden fences
And trees that crowd the track
Night picks another quarrel
And wind must answer back.

ЗОЛОТАЯ ОСЕНЬ

Осень. Сказочный чертог,
Всем открытый для обзора.
Просеки лесных дорог,
Заглядевшихся в озера.

Как на выставке картин:
Залы, залы, залы, залы
Вязов, ясеней, осин,
В позолоте небывалой.

Липы обруч золотой
Как венец на новобрачной;
Лик березы под фатой,
Подвенечной и прозрачной.

Погребенная земля
Под листвой в канавах, ямах.
В желтых кленах флигеля,
Словно в золоченых рамах.

Где деревья в сентябре
На заре стоят попарно,
И закат на их коре
Оставляет след янтарный;

Где нельзя ступить в овраг,
Чтоб не стало всем известно —
Так бушует, что ни шаг,
Под ногами лист древесный;

Где звучит в конце аллей
Эхо у крутого спуска,
И зари вишневый клей
Застывает в виде сгустка.

GOLD AUTUMN

The fairy-tale palace of autumn
Is open to view.
Roads slash through forest
And gaze into lakes.

Hall upon hall
The picture galleries
Of elm, ash, aspen
Astound with gold leaf.

The lime gets married
In a gold tiara,
The silver birch
Wears a wedding veil.

Leaves bury earth
In holes and ditches.
Yellow maples
Gilt-frame the houses.

September trees
Stand pair by pair
At dusk, bark amber
With remains of sunset.

Walk in the gully,
The whole world knows;
The fallen leaves
Storm at your step.

Your steep descent
Echoes down avenues.
Cherry-glue[1] twilight
Chills to clotted blood.

Осень. Древний уголок
Старых книг, одеж, оружья,
Где сокровищ каталог
Перелистывает стужа.

Autumn's a junk-heap:
Clothes, books, weapons.
Jack Frost leafs
The list of treasures.

НЕНАСТЬЕ

Дождь дороги заболотил.
Ветер режет их стекло.
Он платок срывает с ветел
И стрижет их наголо.

Листья шлепаются оземь.
Едут люди с похорон.
Потный трактор пашет озимь
В восемь дисковых борон.

Черной вспаханною зябью
Листья залетают в пруд
И по возмущенной ряби
Кораблями в ряд плывут.

Брызжет дождик через сито.
Крепнет холода напор.
Точно все стыдом покрыто,
Точно в осени — позор.

Точно срам и поруганье
В стаях листьев и ворон
И дожде и урагане,
Хлещущих со всех сторон.

DIRTY WEATHER

Rain cuts glass roads, flooded
With rain, and rips to shreds
The head-scarf of the willows
To shave the willows' heads.

A sweating tractor ploughs
Eight-bladed. Wet leaves fall,
Slapping the earth. Mourners
Drive home from a funeral.

Flying across black furrows
To pond, leaves take their station
As ships of the line; the water
Ruffles with indignation.

The cold puts on the pressure.
Refined through a sieve of air,
Rain drizzles. All the world's
Ashamed of its autumn wear,

Outraged at the sacrilege
Of flocks of leaves and crows
And humbled by the gales
Under a rain of blows.

ТРАВА И КАМНИ

С действительностью иллюзию,
С растительностью гранит
Так сблизили Польша и Грузия,
Что это обеих роднит.

Как будто весной в Благовещенье
Им милости возвещены
Землей в каждой каменной трещине,
Травой из под каждой стены.

И те обещанья подхвачены
Природой, трудами их рук,
Искусствами, всякою всячиной,
Развитьем ремесл и наук;

Побегами жизни и зелени,
Развалинами старины,
Землей в каждой мелкой расселине,
Травой из под каждой стены;

Следами усердья и праздности,
Беседою, бьющей ключем,
Речами про разные разности,
Пустой болтовней ни о чем;

Пшеницей в полях выше сажени,
Сходящейся над головой,
Землей в каждой каменной скважине,
Травой в половице кривой;

Душистой, густой повиликою,
Столетьями, вверх по кусту,
Обвившей былое великое
И будущего красоту;

GRASS AND STONES

So skilfully confusing
Granite and vegetation,
The world and its illusion,
Poland and Georgia

Make twins. On Lady-day
The earth from cracks in stones,
The grass from under walls
Promised these countries grace:

A promise kept by nature
And kept by works of hands,
By art and craft, expansion
Of industry and science;

By sprouting life and leaf,
By ruins of the past,
Earth between stones and grass
That underlines each wall;

By effort and idleness,
By rivers of talk pulsing
With purpose and by talk
That couldn't matter less;

By wheatfields seven foot deep
In over-arching wheat,
By earth in stony footholds
And grass in crooked floorboards;

By scented convolvulus,
Massive, centuries-long,
Winding the bushes, winding
Old greatness, future finery;

Сиренью, двойными оттенками
Лиловых и белых кистей
Пестреющей между простенками
Осыпавшихся крепостей.

Где люди в родстве со стихиями,
Стихии в соседстве с людьми,
Земля в каждом каменном выеме,
Трава перед всеми дверьми.

Где с гордою лирой Мицкевича
Таинственно слился язык
Грузинских цариц и царевичей
Из девичьих и базилик.

By lilac in two colours,
Bunches of white and purple,
Brilliant in corridors
That crumble through old forts;

Where man is nature's cousin
And nature man's good neighbour,
The earth in stony crannies,
The grass at every door;

Where proud Mickiewicz[1] streams
Mysterious with the language
Of Georgian kings and queens,
The minster, the servants' hall.

НОЧЬ

Идет без проволочек
И тает ночь, пока
Над спящим миром летчик
Уходит в облака.

Он потонул в тумане,
Исчез в его струе,
Став крестиком на ткани
И меткой на белье.

Под ним ночные бары,
Чужие города,
Казармы, кочегары,
Вокзалы, поезда.

Всем корпусом на тучу
Ложится тень крыла.
Блуждают, сбившись в кучу,
Небесные тела.

И страшным, страшным креном
К другим каким-нибудь
Неведомым вселенным
Повернут млечный путь.

В пространствах беспредельных
Горят материки.
В подвалах и котельных
Не спят истопники.

В Париже из под крыши
Венера или Марс
Глядят, какой в афише
Объявлен новый фарс.

NIGHT

Night runs with no hitches,
Melting. A pilot
Makes for the clouds
Above a sleeping world,

Drowns in a whirlpool
Of vapour, dwindles
To a cross-stitch,
A mark on linen.

Below are foreign cities,
All-night bars,
Barracks, boilermen,
Stations, trains.

The shadow of wings
Lies flat on clouds,
The stars
Cluster, drift.

Sickeningly
The Milky Way
Heels over to other
And unknown worlds.

In limitless spaces
Continents burn,
Boilermen watch
In basement boiler-rooms.

Under Paris eaves
Mars or Venus
Peers at the posters
That name the new farce,

Кому-нибудь не спится
В прекрасном далеке
На крытом черепицей
Старинном чердаке.

Он смотрит на планету,
Как будто небосвод
Относится к предмету
Его ночных забот.

Не спи, не спи, работай,
Не прерывай труда,
Не спи, борись с дремотой,
Как летчик, как звезда.

Не спи, не спи, художник,
Не предавайся сну.
Ты — вечности заложник
У времени в плену.

While, sleepless, a man
In the splendid distance
Peers from his ancient
And tile-roofed attic

At Venus or Mars,
As if the heavens
Touched on the theme
Of his nightly worries.

Work; watch;
Don't waver; work.
Wrestle with sleep
Like planet and pilot.

There's no surrender
To sleep, artist,
Eternity's hostage,
Captive to time.

ВЕТЕР
(Четыре отрывка о Блоке)

I

Кому быть живым и хвалимым,
Кто должен быть мертв и хулим,
Известно у нас подхалимам
Влиятельным только одним.

Не знал бы никто, может статься,
В почете-ли Пушкин, иль нет,
Без докторских их диссертаций,
На все проливающих свет.

Но Блок, слава Богу, иная,
Иная, по счастью, статья.
Он к нам не спускался с Синая,
Нас не принимал в сыновья.

Прославленный не по программе
И вечный вне школ и систем,
Он не изготовлен руками
И нам не навязан никем.

THE WIND

Four fragments about Blok[1]

I

Only the influential yes-men know
    Whom critics are to propagate
      With praise, or criticise
        And liquidate.

Without their Ph.D's to light the world
    And tell us Pushkin was a writer,
      How should we ever know
        He was, poor blighter.

But Blok, thank God, is a different sort of being
    From all those condescending ones
      Who step from Sinai
        To look for sons.

No school or system pickled him alive
    In well-planned glory. What he wrote
      Keeps him, neither cooked up
        Nor stuffed down throat.

Он ветрен, как ветер. Как ветер,
Шумевший в имении в дни,
Как там еще Филька-фалетер
Скакал в голове шестерни.

И жил еще дед-якобинец,
Кристальной души радикал,
От коего ни на мизинец
И ветренник внук не отстал.

Тот ветер, проникший под ребра
И в думу, в течение лет
Недоброю славой и доброй
Помянут в стихах и воспет.

Тот ветер повсюду. Он — дома,
В деревьях, в деревне, в дожде,
В поэзии третьего тома,
В « Двенадцати », в смерти, везде.

II

He blows like the wind
That roared in the country
When Philip the outrider
Galloped six horses

And grandfather Blok
Was a crystal-souled Jacobin;
The gusty grandson
Is more than his match.

For better for worse
Blok's poems remember
That wind, whistling
Through ribs to soul

That blows where it wills,
In trees and houses,
The rain, Book Three,
The Twelve,[1] death, all.

Широко, широко, широко
Раскинулись речка и луг
Пора сенокоса, толо́ка,
Страда, суматоха вокруг.
Косцам у речного протока
Заглядываться недосуг.
Косьба разохотила Блока,
Схватил косовище барчук.
Ежа чуть не ранил с наскоку,
Косой полоснул двух гадюк.

Но он не доделал урока.
Упреки: лентяй, лежебока!
О детство! О школы морока!
О песни пололок и слуг!

А к вечеру туча с востока.
Обложены север и юг.
И ветер жестокий не к сроку
Влетает и режется вдруг
О косы косцов, об осоку,
Резучую гущу излук.

О детство! О школы морока!
О песни пололок и слуг!
Широко, широко, широко
Раскинулись речка и луг.

III

Widely, widely, widely
Spread the river and meadow.
Harvest hustles with reaping
And threshing, heavy work.
The reapers have no leisure
For gazing at the river.
Harvest is catching; Blok,
The squire's son, grabs a scythe,
Lunges, lucky to miss
a hedgehog, carves two snakes,

But hasn't finished his homework;
'Lazybones', they grumble.
Childhood, leadweight of lessons
And singing from the fields.

Clouds in the east, at evening;
North and south in battle.
A wind, savage, unseasonal
Hurtles against the scythes,
Bleeds on the blades of rushes
That crowd the bending river.

Childhood, leadweight of lessons
And singing from the fields.
Widely, widely, widely
Spread the river and meadow.

Зловещ горизонт и внезапен,
И в кровоподтеках заря,
Как след незаживших царапин
И кровь на ногах косаря.

Нет счета небесным порезам,
Предвестникам бурь и невзгод,
И пахнет водой и железом
И ржавчиной воздух болот.

В лесу, на дороге, в овраге,
В деревне или на селе
На тучах такие зигзаги
Сулят непогоду земле.

Когда ж над большою столицей
Край неба так ржав и багрян,
С державою что-то случится,
Постигнет страну ураган.

Блок на небе видел разводы.
Ему предвещал небосклон
Большую грозу, непогоду,
Великую бурю, циклон.

Блок ждал этой бури и встряски.
Ее огневые штрихи
Боязнью и жаждой развязки
Легли в его жизнь и стихи.

IV

Abrupt horizons menace
The unhealed twilight, bruised
And bleeding like the scar-crossed
　Legs of the reaper.

The sky has many gashes,
Gale-warnings of disaster.
The marshes smell of rust,
　Water and iron.

On roads, in woods and gullies,
In big and little hamlets,
These cloud-inscribing zigzags
　Promise a downpour.

But purple-rusting rims
About a capital city
Mean state events, the cyclone
　Poised for attacking.

Blok saw these patterned heavens
And knew their prophecy.
He waited; the ugly weather
　Gathered its forces,

Blew up, concussed the earth
And signed his life and poems
In flaming strokes, with a frightened
　Thirst for the outcome.

ДОРОГА

То насыпью, то глубью лога,
То по прямой за поворот,
Змеится лентою дорога
Безостановочно вперед.

По всем законам перспективы
За придорожные поля
Бегут мощеные извивы,
Не слякотя и не пыля.

Вот путь перебежал плотину,
На пруд не посмотревши вбок,
Который выводок утиный
Переплывает поперек.

Вперед то под гору, то в гору
Бежит прямая магистраль,
Как разве только жизни впору
Все время рваться вверх и вдаль.

Чрез тысячи фантасмагорий
И местности и времена,
Через преграды и подспорья
Несется к цели и она.

А цель ее — в гостях и дома —
Все пережить и все пройти,
Как оживляют даль изломы
Мимоидущего пути.

THE ROAD

Up hill, down dale,
In loops and flashes,
The endless ribbon
Of road unreels;

Law-abiding
By laws of perspective,
Brushing the fields,
Raising no dust,

Mixing no mud,
Leaping the pond
Without a glance
For the brood of ducklings.

Hurries down dale,
Up hill, as life
Hurries up hill,
Down dale, brushing

A thousand ghosts,
Times, places, obstacles,
Allies; aiming
To run through, live through

Everything,
At home or out,
As the zigzag road
Quickens the distance.

В БОЛЬНИЦЕ

Стояли как перед витриной,
Почти запрудив тротуар.
Носилки втолкнули в машину,
В кабину вскочил санитар.

И скорая помощь, минуя
Панели, подъезды, зевак,
Сумятицу улиц ночную,
Нырнула огнями во мрак.

Милиция, улицы, лица
Мелькали в свету фонаря.
Покачивалась фельдшерица
Со склянкою нашатыря.

Шел дождь, и в приемном покое
Уныло шумел водосток,
Меж тем как строка за строкою
Марали опросный листок.

Его положили у входа.
Всё в корпусе было полно.
Разило парами иода,
И с улицы дуло в окно.

Окно обнимало квадратом
Часть сада и неба клочок.
К палатам, полам и халатам
Присматривался новичок.

Как вдруг из расспросов сиделки,
Покачивавшей головой,
Он понял, что из переделки
Едва ли он выйдет живой.

IN HOSPITAL

Like window-shoppers
They blocked the pavement.
The stretcher was loaded aboard,
The orderly jumped for his seat.

Lights of the ambulance
Dived into darkness.
Streets bustled by; police
And pavements danced in the beam;

Doors and faces
Gaped; the nurse
Rocked gently to the ride
With her bottle of ammonia.

Filling of endless forms
In the still reception room;
Sadly the gutter
Muttered with rain.

They dumped him by the door;
The ward was full, smelly
With iodine;
A breeze blew in.

Intent, he eyed the floors,
White overalls, a window,
Patch of garden,
Tatter of sky

And guessed in a flash
The meaning of the questions
And nodding heads:
The odds were against his life.

Тогда он взглянул благодарно
В окно, за которым стена
Была точно искрой пожарной
Из города озарена.

Там в зареве рдела застава
И, в отсвете города, клен
Отвешивал веткой корявой
Больному прощальный поклон.

« О, Господи, как совершенны
Дела Твои,» — думал больной,—
« Постели, и люди, и стены,
Ночь смерти и город ночной.

Я принял снотворного дозу
И плачу, платок теребя.
О, Боже, волнения слезы
Мешают мне видеть Тебя.

Мне сладко при свете неярком,
Чуть падающем на кровать,
Себя и свой жребий подарком
Бесценным Твоим сознавать.

Кончаясь в больничной постели,
Я чувствую рук Твоих жар.
Ты держишь меня, как изделье,
И прячешь, как перстень в футляр.»

He gazed at the window
Grateful, where a wall
Flared in the light
Of the bright nocturnal city.

A gate turned red
And in the glow a maple
Waved its wry branch
And bowed to him goodbye.

'How perfect are your ways,
O Lord', he mused, 'men, wall,
Night city, death in the night
And beds in hospital.

I tug my handerchief;
Tears worry a way through
The drowsy sedatives
And blur my sight of you.

It's pleasant, as the light
Gropes for my bed, to see
That both my life and self
Were your rich gifts to me.

I feel your warm hands hold me
Here in the ward, replace
Their handiwork, your ring
Inside death's jewel case.'

МУЗЫКА

Дом высился, как каланча.
По тесной лестнице угольной
Несли рояль два силача,
Как колокол на колокольню.

Они тащили вверх рояль
Над ширью городского моря,
Как с заповедями скрижаль
На каменное плоскогорье.

И вот в гостиной инструмент,
И город в свисте, шуме, гаме,
Как под водой на дне легенд,
Внизу остался под ногами.

Жилец шестого этажа
На землю посмотрел с балкона,
Как бы ее в руках держа
И ею властвуя законно.

Вернувшись внутрь, он заиграл
Не чью нибудь чужую пьесу,
Но собственную мысль, хорал,
Гуденье мессы, шелест леса.

Раскат импровизаций нес
Ночь, пламя, гром пожарных бочек,
Бульвар под ливнем, стук колес,
Жизнь улиц, участь одиночек.

Так ночью, при свечах, взамен
Былой наивности нехитрой
Свой сон записывал Шопен
На черной выпилке пюпитра.

MUSIC

Two strong men heave like hell
To haul up towering stairs,
Crooked and tight, a piano—
The belfry gets its bell—

Manhandle it as high
Above the sea of city
As tables of the law
On stony Sinai;

A hundred fathoms down
From drawing room and piano,
Deep as the bed of legends,
The rumble of the town.

The fifth-floor tenant stands
Superb on his veranda
As if he held the whole
World in a ruler's hands;

Goes in to build with notes
A High Mass or a forest,
No alien music but
Chorales on his own thoughts.

His rolling improvisation
Carries the streets, the lonely,
Thunder of fire brigade,
Night, rain and conflagration.

So Chopin wrote his dreams
By candle, on the carved
Black desk, and made archaic
The style of earlier themes;

Или, опередивши мир
На поколения четыре,
По крышам городских квартир
Грозой гремел полет Валькирий.

Или консерваторский зал
При адском грохоте и треске
До слез Чайковский потрясал
Судьбой Паоло и Франчески.

Or with a storm of hooves
That raced four generations
Ahead, the Valkyrie
Rode out across the roofs;

Or sad Tchaikovsky shook
The hall to tears in hell's
Huge uproar, with Paolo,
Francesca and their book.

ПОСЛЕ ПЕРЕРЫВА

Три месяца тому назад,
Лишь только первые метели
На наш незащищенный сад
С остервененьем налетели,

Прикинул тотчас я в уме,
Что я укроюсь, как затворник,
И что стихами о зиме
Пополню свой весенний сборник.

Но навалились пустяки
Горой, как снежные завалы.
Зима, расчетам вопреки,
Наполовину миновала.

Тогда я понял, почему
Она во время снегопада
Снежинками пронзая тьму,
Загдядывала в дом из сада.

Она шептала мне: « Спеши! »
Губами, белыми от стужи,
А я чинил карандаши,
Отшучиваясь неуклюже.

Пока под лампой у стола
Я медлил зимним утром ранним,
Зима явилась и ушла
Непонятым напоминаньем.

AFTER THE INTERVAL

Three months past
When the early blizzards
Angrily swooped
On our undefended garden,

I thought I could hide
Like a hermit, completing
My spring collection
With lines about winter.

But snowdrifts of odds and ends
Piled into mountains;
My schedule collapsed,
We were halfway to spring.

Then I knew why winter
Had peered from the garden
In darkness
Riddled with snowflakes

And whispered 'Hurry',
Lips white with cold;
But I sharpened my pencils
And laughed him off, awkwardly.

Dawdling at table
On lamplit mornings
I missed his message;
And winter came and went.

ПЕРВЫЙ СНЕГ

Снаружи вьюга мечется
И все заносит в лоск.
Засыпана газетчица,
И заметен киоск.

На нашей долгой бытности
Казалось нам не раз,
Что снег идет из скрытности
И для отвода глаз.

Утайщик нераскаянный, —
Под белой бахромой,
Как часто нас с окраины
Он разводил домой!

Все в белых хлопьях скроется,
Залепит снегом взор,
На ощупь, как пропоица,
Проходит тень во двор.

Движения поспешные.
Наверное опять
Кому-то что-то грешное
Приходится скрывать.

FIRST SNOW

The snowstorm scurries about,
Piling and polishing,
Muffles the newspaper woman
And rubs the kiosk out.

Not seldom you and I
In our long lives have seen
The snow play secret agent
Bamboozle every eye.

How often, showing no trace
Of guilt, it brought us home
Involved in its white cloak
From some suburban chase.

The whole world hides in white.
A shadow steers for a yard
Modelled in snow, lunging
Like drunkard in the night.

A flurry, and for dead
Certain some wickedness
Once more repeats its pattern,
Once more must hide its head.

СНЕГ ИДЕТ

Снег идет, снег идет.
К белым звездочкам в буране
Тянутся цветы герани
За оконный переплет.

Снег идет, и все в смятеньи,
Все пускается в полет.
Черной лестницы ступени,
Перекрестка поворот.

Снег идет, снег идет,
Словно падают не хлопья,
А в заплатанном салопе
Сходит наземь небосвод.

Словно с видом чудака,
С верхней лестничной площадки,
Крадучись, играя в прятки,
Сходит небо с чердака.

Потому что жизнь не ждет,
Не оглянешься, и — святки.
Только промежуток краткий,
Смотришь, там и Новый Год.

Снег идет, густой — густой.
В ногу с ним, стопами теми,
В том же темпе, с ленью той
Или с той же быстротой
Может быть, проходит время?

Может быть, за годом год
Следуют, как снег идет,
Или как слова в поэме?
Снег идет, снег идет,
Снег идет, и все в смятенье —
Убеленный пешеход,
Удивленные растенья,
Перекрестка поворот.

SNOW

Geraniums reach out
For the small white stars
Of falling snow
Beyond the window.

In the snow's confusion
The world starts to fly,
Crossroads,
Back door and doorstep.

Snow falls and falls
Not in flakes, but a whole
Patch-coated sky,
Stealing down

Like a crank from his garret
Under the rafters,
Playing at hide-and-seek.

Life is impatient.
Caught out by Christmas
You turn to see New Year.

The snowfall thickens.
In step with the snow
As lazy
As rapid
Time passes us by

And year follows year
Like the falling snow
Or the words of a poem.

Snow without end
Unsteadies the world,
White wayfarer,
Crossroads,
Astonished plants.

СЛЕДЫ НА СНЕГУ

Полями наискось к закату
Уходят девушек следы.
Они их валенками вмяты
От слободы до слободы.

А вот ребенок жался к мамке.
Луч солнца, как лимонный морс,
Затек во впадины и ямки
И лужей света в льдину вмерз.

Он стынет вытекшею жижей
Яйца в разбитой скорлупе,
И синей линиею лыжи
Его срезают по тропе.

Луна скользит блином в сметане,
Все время скатываясь вбок.
За ней бегут вдогонку сани,
Но не дается колобок.

TRACKS IN THE SNOW

Snow-booted girls
Have stippled the fields
From village to village
Towards the sunset.

A lemon-juice sunray
Seeps into hollows
Where child clung to mother,
Chills to a pool

Soft as the spillings
From broken eggshells;
The ski-tracks cut it
Criss-cross with blue.

Pancake in cream
The moon slithers sideways,
Tantalising
The pursuing sleigh.

ПОСЛЕ ВЬЮГИ

После угомонившейся вьюги
Наступает в округе покой.
Я прислушиваюсь на досуге
К голосам детворы за рекой.

Я наверно неправ, я ошибся,
Я ослеп, я лишился ума.
Белой женщиной мертвой из гипса
Наземь падает навзничь зима.

Небо сверху любуется лепкой
Мертвых, крепко придавленных век.
Все в снегу, двор и каждая щепка
И на дереве каждый побег.

Лед реки, переезд и платформа,
Лес и рельсы и насыпь и ров
Отлились в безупречные формы
Без неровностей и без углов.

Ночью, сном не успевши забыться,
В просветленьи вскочивши с софы,
Целый мир уложить на странице,
Уместиться в границах строфы.

Как изваяны пни и коряги
И кусты на речном берегу,
Море крыш возвести на бумаге,
Целый мир, целый город в снегу.

AFTER THE SNOWSTORM

The snowstorm drops to silence.
In a country calm with snow,
Across the river, the voices
Of children come and go.

Snow-dazed, perhaps, or dreaming,
Out of my wits, you'd say,
I saw the winter fall
Dead, a white woman of clay.

The skies admire the moulding
Of winter's dead, pursed eyes.
Each twig is made of snow,
Snow-bound each splinter lies.

The ice-packed river, the wood,
Hill, hollow, station, track
Are cast in perfect moulds
That leave no crick or crack.

A night illumination
Bounces me bolt upright
From self-forgetfulness
And from my bed, to write.

I squeeze a world in stanzas:
Snow town and frozen sea
Of roofs; riverside sculpture
Of bush and fallen tree.

ВАКХАНАЛИЯ

Город. Зимнее небо.
Тьма. Пролеты ворот.
У Бориса и Глеба
Свет, и служба идет.

Лбы молящихся, ризы
И старух шушуны
Свечек пламенем снизу
Слабо озарены.

А на улице вьюга
Все смешала в одно,
И пробиться друг к другу
Никому не дано.

В завываньи бурана
Потонули: тюрьма,
Экскаваторы, краны,
Новостройки, дома,

Клочья репертуара
На афишном столбе
И деревья бульвара
В серебристой резьбе.

И великой эпохи
След на каждом шагу —
В толчее, в суматохе,
В метках шин на снегу;

В ломке взглядов — симптомах
Вековых перемен,
В наших добрых знакомых,
В тучах мачт и антенн;

BACCHANALIA

Winter sky.
Night city. Gates.
Lights and a service
At Boris and Gleb.[1]

Foreheads at prayer,
Vestments, cloaks,
Old women, weakly
Lit by candles.

Street and blizzard
One big kerfuffle;
Not a man
Breaks through to his neighbour.

The howling snowstorm
Drowns the prison,
Cranes and scaffolding,
Diggers and houses,

Tatters of repertoire
Hanging from hoardings,
Filigree silver
Of boulevard trees.

At each step, traces
Of a brave new world:
In stamping crowds,
In tyre-marks on snow,

In shattered opinions
(A sign of huge progress)
In our good friends,
In clouds of aerials,

На фасадах, в костюмах,
В простоте без прикрас,
В разговорах и думах,
Умиляющих нас.

И в значенье двояком
Жизни, бедной на взгляд,
Но великой под знаком
Понесенных утрат.

*   *   *

« Зимы », « Зисы » и « Татры »,
Сдвинув полосы фар,
Подъезжают к театру
И слепят тротуар.

Затерявшись в метели,
Перекупщики мест
Осаждают без цели
Театральный подъезд.

Все идут вереницей,
Как сквозь строй алебард,
Торопясь протесниться
На Марию Стюарт.

Молодежь по записке
Добывает билет
И великой артистке
Шлет горячий привет.

*   *   *

In clothes, façades,
Rugged simplicity,
Moving talk,
Moving thought

And life's double meaning:
Poor; but great
Beneath the sign
Of loss endured.

*　　*　　*

Lights converge on the theatre: Zims, Zisses
And Tatras,[1] a pavement-blinding cavalcade.
Lost in the blizzard, black market ticket sellers
Prolong the uselessness of their blockade.

We jostle in to Mary Queen of Scots[2]
Through ranks as close as ranks of halberdiers.
Young people change their vouchers for a ticket
And greet the actress with a blaze of cheers.

*　　*　　*

За дверьми еще драка,
А уж средь темноты
Выростают из мрака
Декораций холсты.

Словно выбежав с танцев
И покинув их круг,
Королева шотландцев
Появляется вдруг.

Всё в ней жизнь, всё свобода
И в груди колотье,
И тюремные своды
Не сломили ее.

Стрекозою такою
Родила ее мать
Ранить сердце мужское,
Женской лаской пленять.

И за это, быть может,
Как огонь, горяча,
Дочка голову сложит
Под рукой палача.

В юбке пепельно-сизой
Села с краю за стол.
Рампа яркая снизу
Льет ей свет на подол.

Нипочем вертихвостке
Похождений угар,
И стихи, и подмостки,
И Париж, и Ронсар.

К смерти приговоренной
Что ей пища и кров,
Рвы, форты, бастионы,
Пламя рефлекторов?

Outside the door they're scuffling for a ticket;
From gloom of stage the canvas settings grow.
The Queen of Scots appears, sudden as if
She'd left the dance a minute or two ago.

Her life and liberty pound against her ribs;
Prison can't crack her in its stone duress;
She's born to be restless as a dragonfly,
To capture hearts and hurt with a caress;

And these are the reasons why the fiery queen
Must bow her head to the executioner's hand.
She sits beside a table; a row of footlights
Edges her grey skirt with a brilliant band.

To this coquette, dizzy adventure, Paris,
Ronsard, the stage and verse are all the same,
All nothing. Sentenced, she's careless of food and shelter,
The moated fort and the reflectors' flame.

Но конец героини
До скончанья времен
Будет славой отныне
И молвой окружен.

*   *   *

То же бешенство риска,
Та же радость и боль
Слили роль и артистку
И артистку и роль.

Словно буйство премьерши
Через столько веков
Помогает умершей
Убежать из оков.

Сколько надо отваги,
Чтоб играть на века,
Как играют овраги,
Как играет река,

Как играют алмазы,
Как играет вино,
Как играть без отказа
Иногда суждено,

Как игралось подростку
На народе простом
В белом платье в полоску
И с косою жгутом.

*   *   *

И опять мы в метели,
А она всё метет,
И в церковном приделе
Свет, и служба идет.

Her death's heroic; this keeps her at her prime,
Wraps her in rumour; she's the talk of time.

*   *   *

A common lust for danger, common joy and pain
Have welded role and actress into one.
Across so many years the turbulent leading lady
Gives the dead queen the chance to slip her chain.

It's a rare courage, and the luck is rare,
To play for the centuries as gullies play
And as the river plays, given no choice,
Like wine and diamonds and the girl whose hair

Was plaited in a bun, who wore a stripe on white
And played for simple people on the opening night.

*   *   *

Back to the sweeping
Blizzard, the church
With its lights and service,
A winter sky

Где-то зимнее небо,
Проходные дворы,
И окно ширпотреба
Под горой мишуры.

Где-то пир. Где-то пьянка,
Имениинный кутеж.
Мехом вверх, наизнанку
Свален ворох одеж.

Двери с лестницы в сени,
Смех и мнений обмен.
Три корзины сирени.
Ледяной цикламен.

По соседству в столовой
Зелень, горы икры,
В сервировке лиловой
Семга, сельди, сыры.

И хрустенье салфеток,
И приправ острота,
И вино всех расцветок,
И всех водок сорта.

И под говор стоустый
Люстра топит в лучах
Плечи, спины и бюсты
И сережки в ушах.

И смертельней картечи
Эти линии рта,
Этих рук бессердечье,
Этих губ доброта.

*   *   *

Somewhere; courtyard
Giving on courtyard;
Shop window
In tons of tinsel.

Drinks and high jinks
At a birthday party;
Tumble of overcoats
Fur side up.

Stairs, doors,
Opinions, laughter,
Three baskets of lilac,
Icy cyclamen.

Salads and cheeses,
Mountains of caviar,
Herring and salmon
In purple plates.

Crunch of napkins,
Sharpness of sauce,
Wine of all colours,
Vodkas, all kinds.

Hundred-mouthed chatter.
The chandelier
Floods shoulders, bosoms,
Backs and ear-rings.

Deadlier than grape-shot
The lines of these mouths,
Hands without hearts,
Kindness of lips.

*   *   *

И на эти-то дива
Глядя, как маниак,
Кто-то пьет молчаливо
До рассвета коньяк.

Уж над ним межеумки
Проливают слезу.
На шестнадцатой рюмке
Ни в одном он глазу.

За собою упрочив
Право зваться немым,
Он средь женщин находчив,
Средь мужчин — нелюдим.

В третий раз разведенец
И дожив до седин,
Жизнь своих современниц
Оправдал он один.

Дар подруг и товарок
Он пустил в оборот
И вернул им в подарок
Целый мир в свой черед.

Но для первой же юбки
Он порвет повода
И какие поступки
Совершит он тогда!

                    *   *   *

Средь гостей танцовщица
Помирает с тоски.
Он с ней рядом садится,
Зто ведь — двойники.

One silent fellow drinks the dawn home with brandy,
Fixing these marvels with a maniac eye,
Still sober at sixteen glasses; over him
The drunken mediocre people cry.

Long since, he settled his right to be known as dumb;
But he alone, three times divorced, grey,
Lumpish with men, at home among the women,
Has justified the women of his day,

Put into circulation the gifts of friend and sweetheart
And given them a world in fair exchange;
And even now will break his tether
And stop at nothing for the first skirt in range.

*   *   *

Sits down by a ballerina
Dying of boredom among
The guests; these two are twins;

Эта тоже открыто
Может лечь на ура
Королевой без свиты
Под удар топора.

И свою королеву
Он на лестничный ход
От печей перегрева
Освежиться ведет.

Хорошо хризантеме
Стыть на стуже в цвету.
Но назад уже время
В духоту, в тесноту.

С табаком в чайных чашках
Весь в окурках буфет.
Стол в конфетных бумажках.
Наступает рассвет.

И своей балерине,
Перетянутой так,
Точно стан на пружине,
Он шнурует башмак.

Между ними особый
Распорядок с утра,
И теперь они оба
Точно брат и сестра.

Перед нею в гостиной
Не встает он с колен,
На дела их картины
Смотрят строго со стен.

For two pins she'd lie down,
A queen without a following,
To the executioner's axe.

He shepherds his queen away
To flight of stairs from stoves
And overheated rooms;

It's good to chill your blooms
If you're a chrysanthemum;
Then back to fug and party.

On cups of ashes, litter
Of little paper sweet-wraps
And sideboard stubbed with ends

Dawn rises as he bends
To lace her shoe. Her torso
Is tight-laced like a spring.

They are brother and sister now,
By special early morning
Agreement. Looking down

The drawing room pictures frown
Because he kneels before her,
And kneels, and will not rise.

Впрочем что им, бесстыжим,
Жалость, совесть и страх
Пред живым чернокнижьем
В их горячих руках?

Море им по колено,
И в безумьи своем
Им дороже вселенной
Миг короткий вдвоем.

*   *   *

Цветы ночные утром спят.
Не прошибает их поливка,
Хоть выкати на них ушат.
В ушах у них два-три обрывка
Того, что тридцать раз подряд
Пел телефонный аппарат.
Так спят цветы садовых гряд
В плену своих ночных фантазий.
Они не помнят безобразья,
Творившегося час назад.

Состав земли не знает грязи.
Все очищает аромат,
Который льет без всякой связи
Десяток роз в стеклянной вазе.
Прошло ночное торжество.
Забыты шутки и проделки.
На кухне вымыты тарелки.
Никто не помнит ничего.

But pity, fear and shame
Are nothing to the black magic
In their hot hands; the sea

Is nothing, won't reach their knees;
And one mad minute together
Is dearer than a world.

*   *   *

The night flowers sleep in the morning
And bucketful of water
On bucketful won't shake them
Awake from their garden beds.
With snatches in their ears
Of the thirty times repeated
Song of the telephone,
Their own dreams' prisoners,
They've clean forgotten the barefaced
Deeds of an hour ago.

The earth is innocent
Of dirt. A dozen roses
Pour out, unasked, their cleansing
Scent from a bowl of glass.
Forgotten the night and the party,
The jokes and the junketing;
The plates are all washed up;
No one remembers a thing.

ЗА ПОВОРОТОМ

Насторожившись, начеку
У входа в чащу,
Щебечет птичка на суку
Легко, маняще.

Она щебечет и поет
В преддверьи бора,
Как бы оберегая вход
В лесные норы.

Под нею сучья, бурелом,
Над нею тучи.
В лесном овраге за углом
Ключи и кручи.

Нагроможденьем пней, колод
Лежит валежник.
В воде и холоде болот
Цветет подснежник.

А птичка верит, как в зарок
В свои рулады,
И не пускает на порог
Кого не надо.

За поворотом, в глубине
Лесного лога
Готово будущее мне,
Верней залога.

Его уже не втянешь в спор
И не заластишь.
Оно распахнуто, как бор
Все вглубь, все настежь.

ROUND THE TURNING

Alert, on guard
At the gates of the forest
A bird twitters
Lightly, beckoning,

A singing sentry
Mounting a twig
Between cloud and windfall,
Warden of the woods

Keeping his vigil
Above the warrens.
A spring tumbles
In a hidden gully.

Barricaded
With breakage of branches
The chilly marshes
Bloom with snowdrops.

But while the sentry
Trusts in his trills
To guarantee
Against intruders,

Round the turning
Of a forest defile,
Sure as a pledge,
My future waits,

Not to be hoodwinked
Or drawn to discussion,
Opening as deep
As the gates of the forest.

ВСЕ СБЫЛОСЬ

Дорога превратилась в кашу.
Я иробираюсь в стороне.
Я с глиной лед, как тесто квашу,
Плетусь по жидкой размазне.

Крикливо пролетает сойка
Пустующим березняком.
Как неготовая постройка
Он высится порожняком.

Я вижу сквозь его пролеты
Всю будущую жизнь насквозь.
Все до мельчайшей доли сотой
В ней оправдалось и сбылось.

Я в лес вхожу, и мне не к спеху.
Пластами оседает наст.
Как птице, мне ответит эхо
И целый мир дорогу даст.

Среди размокшего суглинка,
Где обнажился голый грунт,
Щебечет птичка под сурдинку
С пробелом в несколько секунд.

Как музыкальную шкатулку
Ее подслушивает лес,
Подхватывает голос гулко
И долго ждет, чтоб звук исчез.

Тогда я слышу, как верст за пять,
У дальних землемерных вех
Хрустят шаги, с деревьев капит
И шлепается снег со стрех.

FULFILMENT

I crawl along the gutter
    (The roads are nice
And gooey) stirring a porridge
    Of clay and ice.

A shrill jay chatters by;
    The birchwood looms
Empty as scaffolding
    Round unbuilt rooms.

    Exact to the hundredth
Of every inch, I see
Down forest cuttings my future
    Fulfilled for me.

    I take my time;
The world will give me way
And echo answer me
    (It answered the jay).

I break the snow-crust, enter.
The bare, soaked soil sticks through;
    A bird sings muted
    A minute or two;

    The eavesdropping forest
    Carries the song
Of this live music box
Echo by echo along.

    Across five versts
    I hear the trees drip-drop,
Boot crunch past signpost
And snow from roofs fall plop.

ПАХОТА

Что сталось с местностью всегдашней?
С земли и неба стерта грань.
Как клетки шашечницы, пашни
Раскинулись, куда ни глянь.

Пробороненные просторы
Так гладко улеглись вдали,
Как будто выровняли горы,
Или равнину подмели.

И в те же дни, единым духом
Деревья по краям борозд
Зазеленели первым пухом
И выпрямились во весь рост.

И ни соринки в новых кленах
И в мире красок чище нет.
Чем цвет берез светлозеленых
И светлосерых пашен цвет.

PLOUGHING

What's up? Who's rubbed the limits
From earth and sky,
Ploughed the land
As chequered as chessboard,

Levelled the mountains
And swept the plains
To pave the distance
So smooth with harrowed fields?

At a breath, the trees
Flanking the furrows
Grow green with down
And stretch full height.

New maples are spotless;
The world's cleanest colours
Are green of birches
And grey of ploughlands.

ПОЕЗДКА

На всех парах несется поезд,
Колеса вертит паровоз,
И лес кругом смолист и хвоист,
И что то впереди еще есть,
И склон березами порос.

И путь бежит, столбы простерши,
И треплет кудри контролерши
И воздух делается горше
От гари, легмей на откос.

Беснуются цилиндр и поршень,
Мелькают гайки шатуна,
И тенью проплывает коршун
Вдоль рельсового полотна.

Машина испускает вздохи
В дыму, как в шапке набекрень,
А лес, как при царе Горохе,
Как в предыдущие эпохи
Не замечая суматохи,
Стоит и дремлет по сей день.

И где то, где то города
Вдали маячат, как бывало
Куда по вечерам устало
Подвозят к старому вокзалу
Новоприбывших поезда.

Туда толпою пассажиры
Текут с вокзального двора,
Путейцы, сторожа, кассиры,
Проводимки, кондуктора.

THE JOURNEY

Full steam, forest and spinning wheels,
Pine-needles, resin, banks of birches
  And the rails racing ahead

To space the telegraph poles, bluster
The ticket-collector's hair; the air
  Turns bitter with falling ashes.

Piston scurries like the devil
In a flurry of links; a shadow hawk
  Goes drifting down the line.

The engine sighs, its hat of smoke
Cocked sideways, while the dreaming forest
Stands as it stood for old Tsar Peabody,[1]
Noticing nothing of all the commotion,
  Dozing the ages away.

The city looms, as it always loomed
Through dusk to exhausted engines, shunting
  New-comers to age-old platforms.

Out of the station flows a river
Of passengers, guards and engine drivers,
Ticket collectors, ticket sellers
  And signalmen. The train,

Intensely secret, rounds a corner,
Raising the city stone on stone,
Niche and notice, roof and chimney,
Playhouse, clubhouse, flat, hotel,
Squares and avenues, forest of limes,

167

Вот он со скрытностью сугубой
Ушел за улицы изгиб,
Вздымая каменные кубы
Лежащих друг на друге глыб,
Афиши, ниши, крыши, трубы,
Гостиницы, театры, клубы
Бульвары, скверы, купы лип,
Дворы, ворота, номера
Подъезды, лестницы, квартиры,
Где всех страстей идет игра
Во имя переделки мира.

Back yard, front door, gate and staircase;
The numbered lodgings where, in the name
Of recreating the world, the city
Plays all its passions like a game.

ПОСЛЕ ГРОЗЫ

Пронесшейся грозою полон воздух.
Все ожило, все дышит, как в раю.
Всем роспуском кистей лиловогроздых
Сирень вбирает свежести струю.

Все живо переменою погоды.
Дождь заливает кровель желоба,
Но все светлее неба переходы
И высь за черной тучей голуба.

Рука художника еще всесильней
Со всех вещей смывает грязь и пыль.
Преображенней из его красильни
Выходят жизнь, действительность и быль.

Воспоминание о полувеке
Пронесшейся грозой уходит вспять.
Столетье вышло из его опеки.
Пора дорогу будущему дать.

Не потрясенья и перевороты
Для новой жизни очищают путь,
А откровенья, бури и щедроты
Души воспламененной чьей нибудь.

AFTER THE THUNDER

The storm has left the air in a fluster.
Things come to life, draw breath, like Eden.
Spreading a purple-handed cluster
The lilac scoops a stream of freshness.

Things come to life with the shift of weather.
The drainpipe overflows with showers.
Behind black cloud a light sky towers
In range on range of blue on blue.

Still more vigorous than the weather
To wash the world, the artist's hand
Dips life in dyes and issues brand
New legends and realities.

Now fifty years of memory
Recede with the receding storm.
Time to accept another stage;
The century has come of age.

It's not the earthquake that controls
The advent of a different life,
But storms of generosity
And visions of incandescent souls.

ЖЕНЩИНЫ В ДЕТСТВЕ

В детстве, я как сейчас еще помню,
Высунешься, бывало в окно,
В переулке, как в каменоломне
Под деревьями в полдень темно.

Тротуар, мостовую, подвалы
Церковь слева, ее купола
Тень двойных тополей покрывала
От начала стены до угла.

За калитку дорожки глухие
Уводили в запущенный сад,
И присутствие женской стихии
Облекало загадкой уклад.

Рядом к девочкам кучи знакомых
Заходили, и толпы подруг,
И цветущие кисти черемух
Мыли листьями рамы фрамуг.

Или взрослые женщины в гневе
Разругавшись без обиняков,
Выростали в дверях, как деревья
По краям городских цветников.

Приходилось, насупившись букой
Щебет женщин сносить словно бич,
Чтоб впоследствии страсть, как науку,
Обожанье, как подвиг, постичь.

Всем им, вскользь промелькнувшим где либо
И пропавшим на том берегу
Всем им, мимо прошедшим,— спасибо,
Перед ними я всеми в долгу.

WOMEN IN CHILDHOOD

Clear as today I picture myself, a boy,
Head poked through window to survey
A side-street dark as a quarry of stone
At height of day.

Twin rows of poplars plunged the church
In shadow, onion domes and all,
Above the poplar-darkened road and sidewalk,
Basement and wall.

A wicket led through footpaths to a garden,
Neglected, puzzling in
A climate of its own,
Unclear but clearly feminine.

Bunches of little girls
Dropped in on girl-friends, neighbours of ours;
Bunches of cherry
Sponged at the window with a froth of flowers;

And grown-up women stood in doorways,
Too angry, after fishwife rows, to pardon,
As rooted as the trees
That lined the public garden.

You had to grin and bear the twittering lash
Of women's tongues, an education
In passion like a science,
Heroic adoration.

To all those women who flickered here or there
Along my life, and turned another way,
I send my thanks
And own a debt to pay.

ЕИНСТВЕННЫЕ ДНИ

На протяженьи многих зим
Я помню дни солнцеворота,
И каждый был неповторим
И повторялся вновь без счету.

И целая их череда
Составилась мало по малу
Тех дней единственных, когда
Казалось нам, что время стало.

Я помню их наперечет:
Зима подходит к середине,
Дороги мокнут, с крыш течет
И солнце греется на льдине.

И любящие, как во сне,
Друг к другу тянутся поспешней
И на деревьях в вышине
Потеют от тепла скворешни.

И полусонным стрелкам лень
Ворочаться на циферблате
И дольше века длится день
И не кончается объятье.

UNIQUE DAYS

My many winters blaze
With winter solstices,
The endless repetition
Of unrepeatable days

Massing in memory till
The pattern is complete;
Remembered as the time
When time was standing still.

Each detail is precise:
Winter, towards midwinter,
Wet roads and streaming roofs
And sun that basked on ice;

The lovers in a dream
Longing themselves together;
The starling boxes high
In hot trees, wet with steam;

The clock hands in a daze
Of sleep, stuck to the dial;
The days like centuries,
The kisses like the days.

ЗИМНИЕ ПРАЗДНИКИ

Будущего недостаточно,
Старого, нового мало.
Надо, чтоб елкою святочной
Вечность средь комнаты стала.

Чтобы хозяйка утыкала
Россыпью звезд ее платье.
Чтобы ко всем на каникулы
Съехались сестры и братья.

Сколько цепей ни примеривай,
Как ни возись с туалетом,
Все еще кажется дерево
Голым и полуодетым.

Вот, трубочиста замаранней
Взбив свои волосы клубом
Елка напыжилась барыней
В нескольких юбках раструбом.

Лица становятся каменней,
Дрожь пробегает по свечкам
Струйки зажженного пламени
Губы сжимают сердечком.

Ночь до рассвета просижена.
Весь содрогаясь от храпа
Дом, точно утлая хижина
Звякает дверцею шкапа.

Новые сумерки следуют,
День убавляется в росте.
Завтрак проспавши, обедают
Заночевавшие гости.

WINTER HOLIDAYS

Because the time to be
Is short as past and present
We stand the Christmas tree
At the centre of the room,

Eternity ablaze
With starry decorations;
And home for the holidays
Our brothers and sisters come.

Through all its paper chains
And fuss of fancy dress
The Christmas tree remains
Half-naked; but shaking out

A fuzzy ball of hair
And grimy as a sweep,
Puts on a lady's air,
Puffed up, in bell-shaped skirts.

The shivering candle light
Turns faces into stone.
The candles pout; their bright
And streaming lips make hearts.

To clap of cupboard doors
The house jumps, frail as hovel,
And shudders with our snores;
We sit the whole night through.

A new day loses height,
Another twilight gains.
The guests who spent the night
And slept their lunch away,

Солнце садится, и пьяницей
Издали, с целью прозрачной
Через оконницу тянется
К хлебу и рюмке коньячной.

Вот оно ткнулось, уродина,
В снег образиною пухлой
Цвета наливки смородинной
Село, истлело, потухло.

Dine as the drunken sun
Is reaching through the window
In front of everyone
For brandy glass and bread;

Then, monstrous, drops below,
Flushed as liqueur of raspberries
And quenches in the snow
Its ugly, swollen face.

БОЖИЙ МИР

Тени вечера волоса тоньше
За деревьями тянутся вдоль.
На дороге лесной почтальонша
Мне протягивает бандероль.

По кошачьим следам и по лисьим
По кошачьим и лисьим следам
Возвращаюсь я с пачкою писем
В дом, где волю я радости дам.

Горы, страны, границы, озера
Перешейки и материки,
Обсужденья, отчеты, обзоры,
Дети, юноши и старики.

Досточтимые письма мужские!
Нет меж вами такого письма,
Где свидетельства мысли сухие
Не выказывали бы ума!

Драгоценные женские письма!
Я ведь тоже упал с облаков.
Присягаю вам ныне и присно
Ваш я буду во веки веков.

Ну а вы, собиратели марок!
За один мимолетный прием
О какой бы достался подарок
Вам на бедственном месте моем!

GOD'S WORLD

Hairfine, from trees to distance
The evening shadows trail.
A forest road; the postwoman
Meets me with my mail.

Then home along the cat-walks
And home by foxes' tracks
With a bunch of letters; at home
I can let my joy relax.

Mountains and lakes, islands
And continents unfold;
How many reviews, discussions,
Children, young people, old.

Most readable letters of men,
I cite you in evidence;
Your thoughtful paper bears
Dry witness to good sense.

Precious letters of women,
I tumble from the sky
Of my amazement, swear
Allegiance till I die.

As for you, stamp collectors,
What wealth to pick and choose
If you could stand a moment
In my unlucky shoes.

NOTES

Notes on *An Essay in Autobiography*

1. EARLY CHILDHOOD

1. i.e. 10 February 1890. In the nineteenth century the "Old" (i.e. Julian Calendar) lagged 12 days behind the Gregorian Calendar which was not introduced in Russia until 1918. In the twentieth century the difference was 13 days. In these notes, both dates are given until 1918.

2. Wet-nurses stayed with children longer than in the West and were a usual and showy sight when out with their charges, as they wore the national dress including the *Kokoshnik* (diadem embroidered with artificial pearls and many rows of coloured beads).

3. Tverskiye-Yamskiye: literally, Tver coach service streets. The Pipe: Truba Square. Tsvetnoy: Flower Boulevard. There was a flea-market in the Truba. The neighbourhood was one of slums and vice, with whole streets of brothels. (cf. *Doctor Zhivago*, Collins Harvill, pp. 411–12.) See Map on p. 4.

4. Literally: "School of Painting, Sculpture and Architecture." The school was founded in 1832 as an "Art Group", became a college in 1843, and was amalgamated with the Imperial College of Architecture in 1863.

5. Mentioned in guide-books of the period as a lively street with well-to-do private houses and foreign shops. Now called Kirov Street. See Map on p. 4.

6. The fire which broke out immediately after the occupation of Moscow by Napoleon.

7. L. N. Tolstoy.

8. In fact, Tchaikovsky died in November 1893 and Anton Rubinstein in November 1894. The trio, "In memory of the Great Artist", was dedicated to N. Rubinstein (1835–81), a famous conductor and pianist, brother of Anton Rubinstein.

9. On 9 November 1863, thirteen pupils of the Academy of Art, all Gold Medallist candidates, refused to paint a picture on the set subject of "Odin in Valhalla". They formed an Artists' Co-operative Society, and, assisted financially by a rich patron of the arts, Tretyakov, founded in 1870 the Society for Travelling Art

Exhibitions (*Peredvizhniki*). The society, which received ideological support from the writings of V. V. Stasov, undertook to educate the masses by means of exhibitions, held in the capitals and the main cities such as Riga, Kazan, etc. Members of the society included the brothers Vasnetsov, Levitan, V. E. Makovsky, Polenov, Repin, Serov, Surikov. The society deeply influenced contemporary Russian taste; indeed its concept of art as a means of persuasion, its insistence on "realism" and the priority it accorded to content at the expense of form, even now determine the views of most averagely educated Russians.

10. Repin, Myasoyedov, Makovsky, Surikov, Polenov. cf. Notes on persons mentioned in *An Essay in Autobiography*. (For the convenience of the English reader, lists of Russian names which may be unknown to him have occasionally been omitted from the text and included in these notes.)

11. Serov, Levitan, Korovin, Vrubel, Ivanov. (cf. preceding note.)

12. The Union was formed in 1903 by a group of painters who, on average, were twenty years younger than their social-minded predecessors and were more tolerant of modern European influences. A number of them had seceded from the Peredvizhniki.

13. Illustrated weekly published in Petersburg from 1870 to 1918. Its publisher (Adolf Fyodorovich Marx, 1839–1904) made the circulation soar to over 200,000 by printing free supplements of complete editions of Russian and foreign classics. Tolstoy's *Resurrection* was serialised in 1899, Nos. 11 to 52.

14. *Peresylnaya turma*. This queer and uniquely Russian institution appeared under Catherine the Great and has survived the changing social structures and political regimes up to this day. Its primary function was a *temporary* prison for prisoners being deported to Siberia. For, strictly historically speaking, with the exception of a few "state criminals", all prisoners were meant to end up in *Katorga* or exile, and not to be kept in prisons proper. However, under the Soviet regime, it has also served as a temporary prison on the long journey to another, long-term prison.

2. SCRIABIN

1. Known as the "forty forties": a poetic exaggeration as Moscow never had 1600 churches, though in the mid-nineteenth century it had 370, for 380,000 inhabitants.

2. According to a theory which became current after the Grand Dukes of Russia had assumed the title of Tsars, Moscow (the capital of Russia from the fourteenth to the eighteenth century) was the Third Rome. (The "First Rome" was the Roman Empire, the "Second" was the Byzantine Empire.)

3. Saints of the Orthodox Church martyred in Illyria in the second century because they erected a cross on a heathen temple which they had been ordered to build. Their feast day is the 15 August. See Map on p. 4.

4. Saints Peter and Paul Gymnasium, attached to the Moscow Lutheran Church, founded for children of the resident German community, but was also used by many Russian and Russian-Jewish Moscow families.

5. Pyotr Semyonovich Vannovsky (1822–1904), Minister of Education (1901 and 1902), modernised secondary education, putting less stress on ancient languages and more on science.

6. Small furnished country house. The school holidays in Russia last from mid-June to end-August and many middle-class families took *dachas* for the whole of this period. Both Leonid Pasternak and Scriabin were teachers and had equally long holidays.

7. Russian equivalent of "Mr Smith".

8. A character in Griboyedov's comedy, *The Misfortune of being Clever*, which ends with the snob Famusov sighing: "But what will Princess Maria Alexevna say?"

9. 1904–09.

10. *V nochnoye*. It was usual in summer for village children to take horses to night pastures, often far from the village. Turgenev describes such a scene in his story *The Bezhin Meadow*.

11. i.e. roughly 1897–1907.

12. Literally: "harmonic Promethean summer lightnings". Scriabin's *Prometheus, Symphonic Poem on the theme of Fire* (1909–10) was to be accompanied by intricate light effects. Scriabin himself devised and built a complicated projector for this purpose.

3. THE NINETEEN HUNDREDS

1. Because of the strikes and revolutionary disorders which occurred during the Russo-Japanese War of 1904–05, Nicholas II was persuaded by his advisers to issue The Manifesto of 17 October, which promised a constitutional régime. But on the day it was issued a procession of students carrying red flags was attacked by Cossacks; one student was killed. His funeral procession a few days later turned into a mass demonstration by students and workers and that evening Cossacks and "Black Hundreds" (members of the "Union of the Russian People") beat up and killed a number of students. (The "Union" was an organisation formed by reactionary anti-Semitic groups; it agitated for the restoration of autocracy and, with the connivance of the police, organised anti-Jewish pogroms and attacks on students who were a traditionally revolutionary body.)

2. The game market district of central Moscow where the Union recruited its rank and file.
3. The final stage of the conflict, which culminated in the general strike, lasted in Moscow from 9 (22) to 19 December 1905 (1 January 1906).
4. *The Scourge: Bich: the Bugaboo: Zhupel.*
5. An exhibition of Leonid Pasternak's paintings was held in Berlin in spring 1906.
6. 'Pussywillows" (*Verbochki*) was first published in the journal *Tropinka*, No. 6, 1906. *Childhood* (*Detstvo*) appeared in the almanac *Grif*, 1904.
7. These quatrains are taken from poems dated respectively 6 (19) August 1902, 26 October (8 November) 1907, and 4 (17) October 1910.
8. The cycle *The Terrible World* (*Strashny Mir*) belongs to the period 1909–16; the rest of the poems mentioned were written in 1904–05. They reflect Blok's obsession with the big city (Petersburg) and its inhumanity, particularly towards women.
9. Bryusov, Andrey Bely, Khodasevich, Vyacheslav, Ivanov, Baltrushaytis. (cf. Note 10, p. 186.)
10. i.e. between 2 and 10 May 1921.
11. Blok died on 7 August 1921.
12. *Die Geheimnisse* (1785), an unfinished epic poem.
13. Winter of 1903–04.
14. The New Drama Theatre founded by the famous actress and producer, Komissarzhevskaya.
15. Gorky, obliged to emigrate as a result of his revolutionary activities in 1905, had stopped in Berlin on his way to the USA.
16. Pasternak described his first meeting with Rilke in *Safe Conduct* which he dedicated to Rilke's memory. Rilke was in Russia from 27 April to 18 June 1899 (when he first met L. Pasternak) and from 1 May to 22 August 1900. Two letters to Leonid Pasternak are published in Rilke's *Briefe aus den Jahren 1892 bis 1904*, Leipzig, 1939. Another letter (14 March 1926), written after L. Pasternak had emigrated to Germany, is included in Rilke's *Gesammelte Briefe in Sechs Bänden*, Vol. V, Leipzig, 1937.
17. There follow Pasternak's translation of Rilke's poems "Der Lesende" and "Der Schauende" (*Gesammelte Werke*, Vol. III, 1927, pp. 135 and 137–8).
18. The Golden Fleece (*Zolotoye Runo*) was a symbolist monthly, patronised by the millionaire N. I. Ryabushinsky, which appeared in Moscow from 1906 to 1909 and sponsored exhibitions of modern painting. The Knave of Diamonds (*Bubnovy Valet*) was a painters' association which existed from 1910 to 1926. The Donkey's Tail (*Osliny Khvost*) was the name of a group of futurist painters. The

Blue Rose (*Golubaya Rosa*) was an impressionist exhibition held in Moscow in 1907.

19. "Rough diamond" is the nearest English equivalent to *samorodok*, meaning "inbred talent not acquired by upbringing or education" (literally: "nugget").

20. *Musaget* (i.e. Musagetes, Apollo, leader of the Muses) a publishing house, founded 1909; published symbolist review of the same name.

21. Andrey Bely, Stepun, Rachinsky, Boris Sadovsky, Emile Medtner, Shenrok, Petrovsky, Ellis, Nilender. (cf. Note 10. p. 186.)

22. Tolstoy left Yasnaya Polyana in the early morning of 28 October (10 November) 1910, travelling third class by train, and died of pneumonia at the stationmaster's house at Astapovo on 7 (20) November 1910.

23. Tolstoy's widow.

24. The antagonism between Tolstoy's disciples, who surrounded him, and his wife, poisoned his last years and contributed to his decision to leave home.

25. *Pushkin's Duel and his Death* (*Duel i Smert Pushkina*) by P. Y. Shchegolev, 1936 (amended edition). Pushkin married Natalya Nikolayevna, née Goncharova, on 18 February 1831, when she was only sixteen. There were two sons and two daughters of this marriage. Pushkin was killed on 29 January 1837, in a duel with a cavalry officer, George Dantès (1812–95), an adopted son of the Dutch ambassador, whom he suspected of being his wife's lover. The background to this episode has been a ceaseless subject of discussion among Russian writers and literary historians.

26. The argument in the last two paragraphs seems to be that the Tolstoyans misunderstood Tolstoy through treating his view as an abstraction, just as scholars of Pushkin have missed the point of Pushkin by making an abstraction of his case.

27. Here, according to E. V. and E. B. Pasternak, he polemicises against V. Shklovsky. Because, following the tradition and theory of Russian formalism of the Twenties, Shklovsky insisted that this strangeness of Tolstoy's vision was a *method*, and not an inborn quality of his very being.

4. EVE OF THE FIRST WORLD WAR

1. cf. *Safe Conduct* where that summer is described in greater detail.

2. Literally: A way of mispronouncing *r*, which was in vogue among Russian aristocrats from the end of the eighteenth century.

3. The revival of Kant's philosophy by Herman Cohen (1842–1918) and other Marburg philosophers greatly influenced Russian idealist philosophers at the time.

4. Dmitry Samarin's grandfather, Yury Fyodorovich Samarin

(1819–76), was a leader of the late Slavophil movement (opposed to the "Westernisers" who favoured Western influence on Russian culture).

5. Where Pasternak lived from 1936. In his poem "The Old Park", in the collection *On Early Trains* (*Na Rannikh Poyezdakh*), 1941, Pasternak describes a wounded Soviet officer who is brought to a hospital which he recognises as the old country house of his family, the Samarins. The poem seems to refer to a son of Pasternak's friend Dmitry.

6. New Economic Policy, introduced by Lenin in 1921.

7. 1913.

8. Literally: "romantic affection and making myself interesting in extraneous ways" (i.e. ways irrelevant to the content of the poems).

9. Literally: "the West would be disclosed in the manœuvres of storms [or misfortunes] and railway sleepers."

10. A historical monthly published in Moscow, 1863–1917.

11. Some of the early poems, including "Venice" and "The Railway Station", were later thoroughly revised by Pasternak and included in the collected poems published in the Twenties and Thirties.

12. A tributary of the Volga.

13. *Kamerny Teatr*, founded by A. Tairov (1885–1950) in Moscow in 1914 in reaction against the realism of the Stanislavsky Theatre, and closed in 1950 for deviating from the principles of socialist realism.

14. A leading Moscow manufacturer of haberdashery.

15. Einem was a chocolate manufacturer; Ferrein was the largest pharmacological establishment in Russia.

16. In fact, *Plaintain* (*Podorozhnik*) did not appear until 1921. Pasternak must have been reading either *Vecher* (*Evening*), 1912, or *Chotki* (*Rosary*), 1914.

17. The two winters are presumably those of 1915–16 and 1916–17. Pasternak's poems *Uralskiye Stikhi* (*Urals Verses*) first published in 1922, and the chapter in *Doctor Zhivago* describing the country around "Yuryatin" reflect Pasternak's experiences in 1915–17.

18. Literally: 250 versts, i.e. about 170 miles!

19. The action of Pushkin's story *The Captain's Daughter* (1836) takes place during the Pugachov rebellion in 1773–75 in the country south of the districts where Pasternak worked, between the Urals and the Lower Volga. cf. *Doctor Zhivago* in which Zhivago writes sketches of the "Pugachev country" which he has visited.

20. An old-established ordnance factory.

21. *The Contemporary* (*Sovremennik*) appeared in Moscow 1911–15.

22. These are described more fully in *Safe Conduct*.

23. i.e. "Shigalyov methods". Shigalyov is a conspirator in Dostoyevsky's *The Possessed* who "sets out from boundless freedom and

arrives at boundless despotism." According to another member of the conspiracy he says, "everyone must spy and inform on everyone else. Everyone belongs to all and all belong to everyone. All are slaves and equal in their slavery. . . . Cicero's tongue will be cut out, Copernicus will have his eyes gouged out, Shakespeare will be stoned. . . . Slaves must be equal."

24. Sasha: diminutive of Alexander (Fadeyev is addressing himself).

25. A main street in central Moscow.

26. Mayakovsky entered the Fourth Form of the Fifth Moscow High School in August 1906 and left the school by his own wish in March 1908.

27. *Prostoye kak Mychaniye*, published in 1916 by the "Parus" publishing house directed by Gorky.

28. Passage quoted from the Holy Week liturgy of the Orthodox Church.

29. The second half of Pushkin's "Desert Fathers" (1836) is a paraphrase of a penitential prayer of St Ephraim of Syria which is recited at all the services in Lent in the Eastern Church. "Troparion", a part of A. Tolstoy's *St John Damascene* (1858), paraphrases the *idiomela* of St John Damascene which forms part of the Orthodox Requiem. Both Pushkin's and Tolstoy's poems have been translated by Maurice Baring.

30. Ivan is the stock fool of Russian folk-lore. Prince Ivan with his friend and adviser, the Grey Wolf, is a character in the folk-tale "The Fire Bird".

31. "*LEvy Front Iskustva*" (Left Front of Art), an association of futurists formed in the early days of the revolution; its journal *Lef* was published 1923–25 and revived for a short time in 1927–28 as *Novy Lef* (*New Lef*).

32. The first volume of the first (unexpurgated) version of M. A. Sholokhov's novel *And Quiet Flows the Don* appeared in 1928; Pilnyak's *The Naked Year* in 1922 and his *Story of the Unextinguished Moon* in 1927; Babel's *Cavalry* in 1924; Fedin's *Cities and Years* in 1924; Vsevolod Ivanov's *Armoured Train No. 14–69* in 1922 and his *Blue Sand* in 1923.

33. There are friendly references to Pasternak in Mayakovsky's speeches as late as 1927. The final break seems to have come during the short life of *Novy Lef*.

34. Supreme Council of People's Economy (*Vysshy Soviet Narodnogo Khozyaystva*), set up in 1917 as supreme economic organ of the dictatorship of the proletariat, and reorganised in 1932 as three bodies: The People's Commissariats of Heavy Industry, Light Industry and Timber Industry.

35. Both by Stalin.

36. First Writers Congress, August 1934.

5. THREE SHADOWS

1. Ehrenburg praised Tsvetayeva's poetry in *Literaturnaya Moskva*, 1956, pp. 709–15. An editorial note to his article announced the forthcoming publication of Tsvetayeva's verse by the State Literary Publishing House; the decision to publish it was confirmed by Surkov in May 1957 and the book has since appeared in several editions.

2. Years immediately following the Revolution.

3. International Congress of Anti-Fascist Writers, 21–25 June 1935. The Soviet delegation included Boris Pasternak, Alexey Tolstoy, I. Ehrenburg, N. S. Tikhonov, Vsevolod Ivanov and others.

4. Zinaida Neuhaus.

5. Gorky suggested in *Pravda* (31 August 1934) that a group of Russian writers including Pasternak should go to Georgia and arrange for the translation of works by Georgian poets into Russian. Pasternak has since published a number of such translations, e.g. *Gruzinskiye Liriki* (*Georgian Lyrical Poets*) 1935, reprinted 1937, *Gruzinskiye Poety* (*Georgian Poets*), 1946, and in *Krasnaya Nov*, 1934, No. 6, pp. 3–5, and *Novy Mir*, 1956, No. 7, pp. 90–2, translations of Yashvili, Leonidze and Tabidze.

6. In a hitherto unpublished poem, "Grass and Stones", Pasternak again compares Georgia and Poland.

7. A suburb of Tiflis.

6. CONCLUSION

1. Pasternak's autobiographical essay was to be published in Russia with a collection of his poems, but the book did not appear in his lifetime. (See Introduction, p. vii.)

Notes on persons mentioned in
An Essay in Autobiography

AKHMATOVA, Anna, pen name of Anna Arkadyevna Gorenko, 1889–1966. *Poet*. Born in St Petersburg. Moved to Crimea with her mother after her parents separated in 1905. Educated in Kiev. Married Gumilyov in 1910, divorced in 1918. First book, *Evening* (1912), warmly received. Second book, *Rosary* (1914), established popularity. Two further collections, *White Flock* (1917) and *Plantain* (1921), appeared in the early years of the Revolution, but afterwards, apart from some important studies of Pushkin, published nothing between *A.D. MCMXXI* in 1923 and 1940. Greater leniency towards writers during the Second World War allowed a severely censored selection of old and new poems (*From Six Books*) to appear. Zhdanov's attack on her in 1946 led to her expulsion from the Union of Soviet Writers. Published patriotic verse in 1950 in an effort to protect her son who was in a labour camp. At the end of her life, a collected (less severely censored) edition of her work appeared under the title *The Flight of Time* (1965). She died in 1966. Her conversation during the period when her two greatest works, *Requiem* (Munich, 1963) and *Poem without a Hero* (the Hague, 1973) were being composed (1938–66), was recorded by Lydia Chukovskaya and is being published in English in three volumes as *Conversations with Akhmatova*.

(*Acmeism* was a movement in Russian poetry which arose in 1912 as a reaction against the mysticism and vagueness of symbolist poetry. It called for a return to clarity, precision and concreteness. The major figures were Akhmatova, Gumilyov, and Mandelstamm.)

"ALKONOST". Publisher of Blok's works. Vol. II of the collected works appeared in Petrograd in 1922. (*Alkonost*: magic bird with a human face in Russian folk-lore.)

ANDREYEVA, Marya Fyodorovna, 1872–1953. *Actress*. Joined Stanislavky's amateur theatrical group in 1894 and later became member of the Moscow Arts Theatre. From 1903, associated with Gorky, acting as his secretary, and travelling with him in Europe and USA. Helped to organise Petrograd Bolshoy Theatre in 1919.

ANISIMOV, Yulian, 1889– . *Poet, critic and translator*.

ANNENSKY, Innokenty Fyodorovich, 1856–1909. *Poet* and eminent classical scholar. Headmaster of famous Tsarskoe-Selo boarding-school (*lyceum*). Translated Rimbaud, Baudelaire, and the whole of Euripedes. In 1904, at the age of forty-eight, he published, under the pseudonym Nik T-o (*nikto*: "nobody"), a book of lyrical poems, *Quiet Songs*, which roused great interest among the symbolist poets of the time. His second book *The Cypress Chest,* published posthumously in 1910, is usually considered to be his masterpiece. The theme of death predominates in his poetry which is constructed with great subtlety and precision. His poetic use of colloquial language foreshadows Pasternak.

ASEYEV, Nikolay Nikolayevich, 1889–1963. *Poet* of the same futurist group as Mayakovsky, whom he distinguished sharply from such futurists (cf. below) as Khlebnikov. Began writing in 1913; published collections of verse during the First World War and revolutionary verses during the Civil War. Helped to found the journal *LEF* in 1923. In 1926 published notable poem on a revolutionary theme, *The Twenty-six* (i.e. the 26 Baku Commissars executed in 1918). Awarded Stalin Prize for poem in honour of Mayakovsky (1941). Wrote patriotic verses in 1941–45 and anti-American verses and songs after the war.

(Russian *Futurism* was a poetic movement initiated by Khlebnikov and Burlyuk who, with Mayakovsky and others, published in 1912 a Manifesto entitled *A Slap in the Face of Public Taste.* The futurists, attracted by technology and other features of modern life, not only reacted against symbolism, particularly its mysticism and æstheticism, but wished to scrap the whole cultural tradition of the past and used shock tactics to bring their ideas to the attention of the public. Their journal *LEF* was intended to counteract the tendency towards a return to conservative realism.)

BABEL, Isaak Emanuilovich, 1894–1938. *Short story writer.* Born in Odessa. First stories published by Gorky in his *Annals* (1915). They were attacked as pornographic and Babel was prosecuted. Fought with Budyony's Cossack cavalry in Soviet-Polish war. Stories of early Soviet period began to appear in 1923 and won him recognition as an outstanding writer. Wrote on Polish campaign (*The Red Cavalry,* 1923) and about Odessa underworld; stories of blood and death, crime, heroism and cruelty; his irony enhances their heroic pathos. Disappeared in purge of 1937–38. In 1956 his work was re-published and discussed in Russia for the first time since 1937.

BAGRITSKY, Eduard Georgyevich, pen-name of Dzyubin, 1895–1934. *Poet.* One of the most gifted post-revolutionary poets. Wrote verses during the First World War influenced by Mayakovsky, Gumilyov and acmeism (cf. note on AHKMATOVA). Verses in the Twenties deal with Civil War and life of sailors and fishermen. The setting of his major work, "The Epic of Apanas" (1926), is the Civil War in the Ukraine. Poems in the Thirties praise the constructive work of ordinary people ("The New Knights") and especially of Soviet young people ("Death of a Pioneer Girl").

BALMONT, Konstantin Dmitryevich, 1867–1943. *Poet*. Leader of early symbolist movement. First collection of poems was published in 1894. Travelled in South Africa, Mexico, New Zealand, Spain. Translated Shelley, Whitman, E. A. Poe, Calderon. Emigrated in 1918 and died in Paris.

BALTRUSHAYTIS, Jurgis Kazimirovich, 1873–1945. *Poet*. Born in Lithuania, son of a peasant. Taught to read by village priest, then went to school, keeping himself from the age of fifteen as teacher in winter and shepherd in summer. Studied at Moscow University. Travelled in Europe and America. In 1921 became Lithuanian Chargé d'Affaires in Moscow. From 1899, wrote poetry in Russian and Lithuanian. Associated with symbolists and co-founder of their publishing house "Scorpion". Translated Byron, Ibsen, D'Annunzio, Hamsun, Wilde and Strindberg.

BELINSKY, Vissarion Grigoryevich, 1811–48. A famous *literary critic* whose ideas on the social purpose of literature greatly influenced contemporary Russian writing. First critic to appreciate Dostoyevsky. Because of his passionately polemical disposition, was nicknamed by his friends "Furious Vissarion".

BELY, Andrey, pen-name of Boris Nikolayevich Bugayev, 1880–1934. *Poet* and *novelist*. Born in Moscow, son of a professor of mathematics. Influenced by Vladimir Solovyov's mystical teaching, Bely believed that the first years of the new century were to bring a new revelation – that of the feminine hypostasis, Sophia – and that its coming would transfigure the world. His first writings, already showing the musical construction of his prose at its best, appeared in 1902, under the title *Symphony (Second, Dramatic)*; this "Second" Symphony was followed by the *First* (1904), *Third* (1905) and *Fourth* (1908). In 1904 he began to contribute to Bryusov's journal *The Scales*. Published two novels, *The Silver Dove* (1909) and the more famous *Petersburg* (1913), which were to have an enormous influence on early Soviet prose. 1912–16: lived at Rudolf Steiner's anthroposophic centre in Switzerland, working on the construction of an anthroposophic temple and writing. On returning to Russia published *Kotik Letayev* (1917). Welcomed the Bolshevik revolution as a destructive and emancipating storm. 1918–21: engaged in many activities which included the founding of a Free Philosophical Association, courses for proletarian poets and innumerable lectures. Spent one year in Berlin (1922–23), then returned to Russia.

Though a lesser poet than Blok, Bely was perhaps the most

original and influential of the symbolists. A recognised master of metre and rhythm, he was also an important literary critic and an original theorist of Russian prosody.

BLOK, Alexander Alexandrovich, 1880–1921. Probably the greatest *poet* of the "silver age" of Russian literature, and of the symbolist movement; worshipped by young people in Russia before the revolution. Began writing very early. Contributed to symbolist journal *The Golden Fleece*. In 1904 published *Verses about the Beautiful Lady*, poems of mystical love for a being whom Blok identified with the feminine hypostasis of the Deity. Soon, however, his poetry became more pessimistic and more earthy. In "The Stranger" (1904–8) he is preoccupied with the social conflict and with the image of the Unknown Woman which has replaced that of the Beautiful Lady. The cycle "The Field of Kulikovo" (1908) shows Blok's sensitiveness to Russia's destiny, which verged on prophecy. He welcomed the Bolshevik revolution as a cleansing storm and as the expression of Russia's elemental soul. This concept found expression in his famous poem "The Twelve" (1918), an apocalyptic vision of the revolution personified by twelve Red Army men, apostles of the new world, led by Christ crowned with a wreath of white roses, and patrolling the streets of Petrograd. But Blok's enthusiasm soon waned. After "The Scythians" (written in January 1918 and expressing Russia's "love-hatred" of the West) he wrote little else and died, a disillusioned man, three years later.

BOBROV, Sergey Pavlovich, 1889–1971. *Poet.* Leader of futurist "Centrifugue group" and author of works on versification and theory of literature. His prose tale *The Revolt of the Misanthropes* is, like Zamyatin's more famous *We*, a horrifying vision of the collectivist future.

BRYUSOV, Valery Yakovlevich, 1873–1924. *Poet.* Born in Moscow, grandson of a serf, son of a rich merchant of radical views. Studied at Moscow University. In the Nineties read Baudelaire, Verlaine, Mallarmé. In 1894–95 edited *Russian Symbolists*. In 1895 published his own poems, provocatively called *Chefs d'œuvres*, and was attacked as a decadent. Became editorial secretary to journal *Russian Archive* (1903), then to *New Way*. Worked with publishing firm Scorpion which published his *Tertia Vigilia* and *Urbi et Orbi*. Editor of journal *The Scales* published by Scorpion (1904–09) and literary editor of *Russian Thought* (1910–12). Became war correspondent in 1914. Wrote poem to Gorky in 1917. Joined Bolsheviks in 1919; founded Literary and Art Institute in 1921. Died of typhus. Published some eighty books in his lifetime, including translations of Verhaeren, Maeterlinck, E. A. Poe, Goethe, Virgil, etc., some historical novels, and works on Pushkin, Gogol, Tyutchev, etc. Introduced free verse into Russian poetry and was the first to use peasant dance tune rhythm (*chastushki*). A cold academic poet who made important contributions to the technique of Russian prosody; Andrey Bely spoke of him as "the poet of marble and bronze".

CHIKOVANI, Simon Ivanovich, b. 1902. *Poet*. Glorified the revolution in Georgia. Awarded Stalin Prize in 1947.

DROZHZIN, Spiridon Dmitryevich, 1848–1930. *Poet*. Of peasant origin. Began publishing verse in 1873. From 1896 lived in his native village in Tver province, farming and writing. Influenced by Nekrasov. Depicted hardships of peasant life. Welcomed revolution. Wrote "In Memory of Lenin" (1924).

DURYLIN, Sergey Nikolayevich, 1877–1954. *Poet. Critic*. Pseudonyms: S. Severny, S. Rayevsky. In 1916 wrote study on Lermontov from standpoint of Andrey Bely's theories. Important later books: *Repin and Garshin* (1926), *From Gogol's Family Chronicle* (1928), *About Tolstoy* (1928).

EHRENBURG, Ilya Grigoryevich, 1891–1967. *Novelist*. In 1909 went to Paris and entered the bohemian literary world. First wrote poetry. During the First World War remained in France as war correspondent. Returned to Russia in 1917 and lived in the south under the Whites. In 1921 was arrested by the Soviet authorities, but released when cleared by them. Returned to Paris and stayed mostly in Western Europe until 1941. Was Soviet war correspondent in Spain in 1936–37. During Second World War wrote much patriotic propaganda. First successful novel, *Julio Jurenito* (1922), a satire. *Trust D. E.* (1923), a fantasy of the conquest of Europe by America. *The Second Day* (1933) depicts the construction of a steel works in Siberia and an intellectual's acceptance of Soviet life. His *Storm* and *Ninth Wave* were widely read in England and America. His novel *The Thaw*, written soon after Stalin's death, inolved him in heated polemics with several Soviet writers, especially Konstantin Simonov.

ELLIS-KOBYLINSKY, Lev Lvovich, 1874–1947. *Poet* and *critic*. Member of Society of Religious Philosophy. Emigrated and died in Locarno.

ENGEL, Yuly Dmitryevich, 1868–1927. Leading *writer* on musical subjects and *composer*. Studied at Moscow Conservatoire. From 1897 in charge of music column in *Russian News*. One of the founders of the People's Conservatoire (1906) and of the Society for Jewish Folk Music (1908). First biographer of Scriabin (1916). After 1917 active in musical education. Emigrated to Tel-Aviv in 1924.

FADEYEV, Alexander Alexandrovich, 1901–56. *Novelist*. of peasant origin, grew up in far eastern Siberia. Served on Red side in Civil War. First important work: short novel, *The Rout* (1927), set among partisans in Far East. *The Last of the Udege* (1928–36) depicts changes made by revolution in the life of an almost extinct Far Eastern tribe. Wrote famous war novel *The Young Guard* (1945); re-wrote parts of it after strong Communist Party criticism. 1939–53: Secretary of Union of Soviet Writers. An ardent Stalinist, Fadeyev was strongly criticised by his fellow writers during the "thaw". He committed suicide in 1956.

FEDIN, Konstantin Alexandrovich, 1892–1977. *Novelist.* Member of the Serapion Brotherhood, see below. *Cities and Years* (1924), was one of the earliest attempts to show the impact of the revolution on an intellectual and was attacked by some Soviet critics for its hero's "doubts". The hero of *Brothers* (1928) is an artist whose individualism is again opposed to the obligations of Soviet life. In the Thirties Fedin appeared to have overcome his objections to the Soviet régime. *The Rape of Europe* (1934) contrasts "decadent" Europe with progressive Russia. After the war published *Early Joys* (1945–46) and *Extraordinary Summer* (1948).

(*Serapion Brotherhood:* formed in 1921. Named after the hermit Serapion in Hoffman's *Tales*, in whose cave various people gathered and told their experiences. Besides Fedin the group included Lunts, Tikhonov, Vsevolod Ivanov and others. It helped to bring older writers in touch with younger writers demobilised from the Civil War, and to restore normal literary activity.)

GE (or Gué), Nikolay Nikolayevich, 1831–94. *Painter.* Studied in Italy. Member of Society for Travelling Art Exhibitions. Close friend of Tolstoy. Painted religious, then historic, scenes of great dramatic power (e.g. "The Last Supper", "Peter the Great and the Tsarevich Alexey"). His portraits include those of Turgenev, Nekrasov, Tolstoy, etc. Under Tolstoy's influence went back to religious themes (e.g. "What is Truth", "Crucifixion", etc.).

GLIER, Reingold Moritsovich, 1874–1957. *Composer* and *conductor.* Born in Kiev of musical family. Studied at Kiev College of Music and Moscow Conservatoire. Began conducting in 1908. 1914–20: Director of Kiev College of Music; 1920–41: Director of Moscow Conservatoire. One of the most prominent figures in the Moscow post-revolutionary musical world. Composed ballets including *Red Poppy* (first ballet on revolutionary theme) and *Bronze Horseman.* People's Artist of the USSR. Awarded Order of Lenin and three Stalin Prizes. Prokofyev and other composers were his pupils.

GONCHAROVA, Natalya Sergeyevna, 1883–1962. *Painter.* Influenced by cubism, futurism, Eastern folk art, Henri Rousseau. Married Larionov and tried, with him, to found new theory "Luchism" (*luch:* "ray"). Took part in "World of Art" exhibitions. Went to Paris on Diaghilev's invitation and was responsible for several of his settings including *Coq d'Or.* Exhibited in Paris and America.

GORKY, Maxim, pen name of Alexei Maximovich Peshkov, 1868–1936. Born in Nizhny-Novgorod, now named after him. Play, *The Lower Depths*, triumphant success at Moscow Arts Theatre. Active in revolutionary movement; arrested in 1905, but released following a petition signed by statesmen and fellow writers. While in America wrote his novel *Mother* (1906), regarded as a pioneering work of socialist realism. *The Life of a Useless Man* (1907), his novel about the Tsarist system of spies and informants, was banned in 1908 and again in 1914; only published in Moscow in 1917 after the Revolution. Founded socialist daily newspaper, *New Life*. Went to Italy in 1921, where he completed his autobiographical trilogy, *My Childhood, My Apprenticeship* and *My Universities*. Returned to Moscow as a fellow-traveller in 1928; from then on a champion of the socialist cause. He died in 1936 and was given a hero's funeral in Red Square.

GRIN, Alexander Stepanovich, pen-name of Grinevsky, 1880–1932. *Novelist.* Author of fantastic novels and short stories which enjoyed a tremendous popularity in the Soviet Union.

GUMILYOV, Nikolay Stepanovich, 1886–1921. *Poet.* Principal founder of acmeism (cf. note on AKHMATOVA). Studied in Paris and Petersburg. First book published in Paris in 1905. Married Akhmatova in 1910, divorced in 1918. In 1911 travelled in Abyssinia and Somaliland and remained fascinated by Africa. Only Russian poet to enlist as private in 1914; awarded St George's Cross twice; commissioned in 1915. Was in Paris, as Provisional Government Commissioner for Affairs of Russian Troops in France, when October Revolution broke out; returned to Russia in 1918. Lived in Petrograd, taking part in work of translation initiated by Gorky, teaching younger poets and writing his best verse ("The Pyre", 1918, and "The Pillar of Fire", 1921). Shot for alleged participation in White Guard conspiracy. His poetry, exotic and fantastic, is dominated by his love of adventure.

IVANOV, Sergey Vasilyevich, 1846–1910. *Painter.* Member of Society for Travelling Art Exhibitions.

IVANOV, Vsevolod Vyacheslavovich, 1895–1963. *Novelist* and *playwright.* Associated for a time with Serapion Brotherhood (cf. note on FEDIN). Wrote on Civil War in which he had taken part (*Partisans*, 1921). His play, *Armoured Train* 14–69, was produced by Stanislavsky for Moscow Arts Theatre. Play, *Blockade* (1929), deals with suppression of Kronstadt rising of 1921. Returned to Civil War themes in the Thirties, wrote patriotic articles and stories during Second World War, and in 1947 published *Encounters with Maxim Gorky*. (No relation to Vyacheslav Ivanov.)

IVANOV, Vyacheslav Ivanovich, 1864–1949. *Poet* and classical scholar of great erudition. Born in Moscow, son of a geodesist. Studied at Moscow University but left after two terms for Berlin where he studied history under Mommsen, as well as philology and philosophy. Travelled in Europe, Egypt and Palestine, lived mainly in Italy. The main subject of his research was the Cult of Dionysius and the Origins of Tragedy. Was influenced by Nietzsche and Vladimir Solovyov. Settled in Petersburg in 1905. Wrote for the journals, *Golden Fleece, The Scales, Apollo,* etc. After the revolution was active in education in Moscow, then became professor at Baku University. Emigrated in 1924. Became a Roman Catholic. Died in Rome. Wrote poetry and prose works of which some have been translated (e.g. *Freedom and the Tragic Life,* a study of Dostoyevsky).

KHLEBNIKOV, Velemir (Viktor) Vladimirovich, 1885–1922. *Poet.* Founder of Russian futurism and co-author of futurist manifesto, *A Slap in the Face of Public Taste* (cf. note on ASEYEV). One of the most eccentric and controversial figures of modern Russian literature. Born in Astrakhan, son of a civil servant. Came to Petersburg and joined *avant garde* literary circles in 1909. Travelled about Russia, his only luggage an old pillow-case stuffed with MSS. of his poems and calculations intended to establish mathematical laws in history. Served in Tsarist Army, then took part in Red Army campaign in Persia (1920); died in extreme poverty. Had great insight into spirit of Russian language; most modern poets have been influenced by his feeling for words. His first "etymological" poem (1910) consisted of nothing but invented derivatives of the word *smekh* (laughter).

KHODASEVICH, Vladislav Felitsyanovich, 1886–1939. *Poet, critic* and *literary historian.* Published his first poems in 1908 but won general recognition only after publication of post-revolutionary books, *The Way of the Grain* (1920) and *The Heavy Lyre* (1923). His poetry expresses contradiction between the freedom of man's immortal soul and its slavery to matter and necessity. A striking feature of his writing is his poetic wit. Emigrated in 1922, lived in Paris and became a brilliant literary critic and expert on Pushkin.

KLYUCHEVSKY, Vasily Osipovich, 1841–1911. Famous *historian.* Professor of Moscow University and at one time Leonid Pasternak's part-time colleague on the staff of the School of Painting, Sculpture and Architecture. His most important work: *Course of Russian History,* 5 vols, published 1904–11.

KOLTSOV, Alexey Vasilievich, 1809–42. *Poet.* Famous for his genuine natural talent for song-like lyrical poetry.

KOMISSARZHEVSKAYA, Vera Fyodorovna, 1864–1910. Famous dramatic *actress.* Began stage career as amateur in 1892; went to the provinces as professional actress in 1893. In 1896 joined the Petersburg Alexandrinsky Theatre. Founded her own theatre in Petersburg in 1904. Sister of famous producer Fyodor Komissarzhevsky.

KOROVIN, Konstantin Alexeyevich, 1861–1939. Landscape *painter,* but particularly famous as designer of scenery for theatre and opera, e.g. *A Life for the Tsar* (1904), *Sadko* (1906), *The Snow Maiden* (1907), Khovanshchina (1912). Later became an impressionist. Died in emigration.

KRYMOV, Nikolay Petrovich, 1884– . *Painter*. Began as journalist, member of "Blue Rose" group. Later turned to realistic landscape painting. Also designed theatre décors.

LEONIDZE, Georgy Nikolayevich, 1899–1966. *Poet*. At first influenced by symbolists. Wrote poems praising Socialist Construction; also about the countryside and history of Georgia. Awarded Stalin Prizes in 1941 and 1952.

LEVITAN, Isaak Ilyich, 1861–1900. *Painter*, famous for his poetic interpretation of Russian landscape. One of Chekhov's closest friends. Painted series of Volga scenes in the Eighties and Nineties. His "Vladimirka" (1892) shows the road followed by exiles to Siberia. In 1888 visited Paris where he discovered the Barbizon painters and impressionists and was influenced by their style.

LOMONOSOV, Mikhail Vasilyevich, 1711–65. *Poet* and *scientist*. Son of Archangel fisherman, ran away from home, walked to Moscow in search of education; rose to be a scientist of European fame and poet of considerable merit; known as "father of modern Russian literature". Read mathematics, physics and philosophy at Marburg (1736–41) under Leibnitz's disciple, Christian Freiherr von Wolff (1679–1754). Wrote on Russian grammar and style.

MAKOVSKY, Sergey Konstantinovich, 1878–1962. *Poet, critic* and editor of St Petersburg review Apollo (1909–17). Emigrated to Paris in 1922.

MAKOVSKY, Vladimir Yegorovich, 1846–1920. *Painter*. Member of the Society for Travelling Art Exhibitions. Prominent in realist revolt against academism. Painted urban scenes emphasising social contrasts. Pictures include "The Condemned" (1879), "Bank Crash" (1881), "Interrogation of a Revolutionary" (1904).

MANDELSHTAMM, Osip Emilyevich, 1892–1938. Acmeist *poet*. Major figure in twentieth-century Russian poetry. Published three small books of poems in his lifetime, *Stone* (1913), *Tristia* (1922) and *Poems* (1928); also essays on Russian civilisation and art and poetry. Had an extensive knowledge of Russian, French and Latin poetry; an original thinker and literary critic. A satirical poem about Stalin led to his exile in Voronezh, where he filled three notebooks in a last creative burst. In 1937 returned to Moscow where he was arrested again. He died in a labour camp near Vladivostok in 1938. His story is told in Nadezhda Mandelshtamm's memoirs, *Hope against Hope* and *Hope Abandoned*.

MARTYNOV, Leonid Nikolayevich, 1905– . *Poet* and *journalist*. From 1922, published poems about the Civil War, and about Siberia and Central Asia.

MAYAKOVSKY, Vladimir Vladimirovich, 1893–1930. *Poet.* The most outstanding figure in Russian futurism (cf. note on ASEYEV). Born in Transcaucasia, son of a forestry official. Joined Bolshevik underground group at fourteen; spent some time in detention. Studied painting and joined newly emerging futurist movement whose revolutionary spirit and universalism attracted him. Signed Futurist Manifesto in 1912. In 1914 published tragedy, *Vladimir Mayakovsky*, in which he shocked the public by comparing himself to Christ. "The Cloud in Trousers" (1915) is a poem of unrequited love. In 1917 Mayakovsky rallied at once to the Soviet régime; wrote *Mystery Buffo* (1918), a verse play prophesying victory of revolution over capitalism. 1918–20: contributed drawings and texts for thousands of propaganda posters. In mid-Twenties travelled in Europe, USA and Latin America, writing poems sharply critical of life under capitalism. But his satirical plays, *The Bed Bug* (1928) and *The Bath House* (1929), reflect disillusionment with growing philistinism and bureaucracy in Soviet life. Joined the Russian Association of Proletarian Writers (RAPP), the agency through which the Party controlled literature in the mid-Twenties, and compared his poetry with "a gigantic hundred volumes Party membership card". But only two months later shot himself without having written another line except his suicide note, in which he said: "the boat of love has crashed on the rocks of everyday life." Responsible communists always saw a dangerous individualism in his verse, but after his death his vogue as "the bard of the revolution" became an established cult.

MEDTNER, Emile Karlovich, 1872–1936. *Philosopher* and *philologist*. Emigrated and died in Dresden.

MURATOV, Pavel Pavlovich, 1881–1950. *Novelist* and *critic*. Associated with "The World of Art". Author of *History of Old Russian Painting* (1914). Emigrated; lived in Dublin; published two books on *The Russian Campaigns* of 1941–43 and 1943–45 (1941 and 1946).

MYASOYEDOV, Grigory Grigoryevich, 1835–1911. *Painter*. Studied abroad. On return to Russia became one of the organisers of the Society for Travelling Art Exhibitions. Paintings deal with peasant life and historical themes. Member of Academy of Art from 1893.

NADIRADZE, Kolau, 1895– . Georgian *poet*. Studied at Moscow University. First verses appeared in 1916 in Georgian symbolist journal *Blue Horns* (cf. note on TABIDZE). His early poetry was mystical and nationalistic. After sovietisation of Georgia, Nadiradze was at first hostile but later wrote on revolutionary themes.

NILENDER, V. O. *Poet* and *translator*. Member of Society of Religious Philosophy.

OLENINA D'ALHEIM, Maria Alexeyevna, 1869–1970. *Singer*. In

1908, founded Moscow music society *Dom Pesni* ("House of Song") which played a notable role in the development of musical taste in Moscow and Petersburg. Wrote *The Legacy of Mussorgsky*. After 1918 lived in Paris.

OSTROVSKY, Alexander Nikolayevich, 1823–86. Famous *playwright*, closely associated with the Maly Theatre in Moscow.

PASTERNAK, Boris Leonidovich, 1890–1960. *Poet* and *novelist*. Born in Moscow, son of painter Leonid Pasternak and pianist Rosa Pasternak (née Kaufman). Childhood spent in Moscow, with frequent visits to paternal grandparents in Odessa. Classical education in Moscow. Meeting with Scriabin in 1903 opened period of intense preoccupation with music. 1906: year in Berlin with family. 1908: Moscow University, faculty of law; later changed to philosophy on advice of Scriabin. 1910–12 involvement with "Serdada" circle and *Musaget* group of writers. Summer 1912: Marburg University, reading neo-Kantian philosophy under Hermann Cohen. An abortive love affair coincided with his abandonment of philosophy and discovery of poetry as his true vocation. Travel to Venice and Florence. 1913: graduated from Moscow University and began first active period of creative work. Spring 1914: joined "Centrifuge", an association of moderate futurists. May 1914: first meeting with Mayakovsky. Autumn 1914: first collection of poetry, *A Twin in the Clouds*. 1914–16: tutor to son of Moscow manufacturer. October 1915: first meeting with Khlebnikov, founder of Russian futurism. 1915–17: exempted from military service on medical grounds, spent two winters doing clerical work in ordnance factories in the Urals. March 1917: returned to Moscow. Second book of poetry, *Above the Barriers*. Summer 1917: wrote third book of poetry, *My Sister, Life* and two stories, *The Childhood of Luvers* and *Letters from Tula*. Winter 1918–19: severe illness. 1920: estrangement from Mayakovsky. May 1921: meeting with Alexander Blok in Moscow. 1921: departure of parents and sisters for Berlin. Work as salesman in Moscow bookshop where he discovered Tsvetayeva's poetry. 1922: *My Sister, Life* published; poetric reputation established. Married to Evgeniya Lourié. Honeymoon in Berlin; visit with parents; preparation of fourth book of poetry, *Theme and Variations*. 1924: short spell of work in library of People's Commissariat of Foreign Affairs. 1925: publication of four stories in book form (*Childhood of Luvers, Letters from Tula, The Mark of Apelles, Aerial Ways*). 1927: publication in book form of two historical "epic" poems, *Nineteen Five* and *Lieutenant Schmidt*. 1927–36: increasing popularity of Pasternak's poetry, published and republished in various editions. 1929–31: serialisation of first autobiography, *Safe Conduct*. 1930-31: friendship with Georgian poet, Paolo Yashvili. Early 1930s: estrangement from wife, divorce and remarriage to Zinaida Nikolayena Neuhaus. Stay in Georgia and work on translations of Georgian poets. 1931: publication of novel in verse, *Spektorsky*, and collection of verse for children, *Zoo*. 1932: publication of new and selected poems, *Second Birth*. 1932–41: silence as a poet. Active work as a translator. August 1934: first Congress of Union of Soviet Writers: Pasternak praised and attacked but generally regarded as master of modern Russian poetry. Mid-Thirties: Move to Peredelkino where he lived for the rest of his life. June 1935: attended first Anti-fascist Congress of Writers in Paris. Meeting with Tsvetayeva and her family 1937: refused to sign document approving of execution of Marshal Tukhachevsky and others. 1937: befriended young playwright, Alexander Afinogenov who had been expelled from the Party and from the Union of Soviet Writers. 1935–37: publication in book form of translations of Georgian poets. Late Thirties: early drafts of novel that became *Doctor Zhivago*. 1941: translation of *Hamlet* published. 1941–45: publication of patriotic war poems and continued work on translations of Shakespeare. 1942: translation of *Romeo and Juliet* published. 1943: publication of new poems from period 1936–44, *On Early Trains*. 1944: translation of *Antony and Cleopatra* published. First meeting with Olga Ivinskaya, who became his lover and mistress and on whom the character Lara in *Doctor Zhivago* is partly based. 1945: translation of *Othello* published together with a collected edition of poems, *Earth's Vastness*. 1946: Zhdanov's savage attack on "cosmopolitanism" in literature imposes renewed silence on Pasternak as a poet. 1950: publication of translations of Goethe's *Faust* and of selected poems by Petöfi. April 1954: publication of ten poems from *Doctor Zhivago* in the journal *Znamaya*, and announcement of novel. Summer 1956: *Doctor Zhivago* submitted to editorial board of *Novy Mir* and rejected in September with ten-page letter of explanation and comment. Autumn: 1957 *Doctor Zhivago* first published abroad in Italy; unsuccessful attempts made by Soviet authorities to prevent publication. New poems published in *Novy Mir*, though planned collected edition of Pasternak's poems, for which *An Essay in Autobiography* was intended as an introduction, abandoned due to publication of *Doctor Zhivago* abroad. 1958: publication of *Doctor Zhivago* in Great Britain and the USA. 1959: acceptance of Nobel Prize for Literature, but Pasternak subsequently forced to renounce the award. 1960: work begun on *Blind Beauty*, a full-length stage play. Death of Pasternak: 30 May 1960.

PASTERNAK, Leonid Osipovich, 1862–1945. Well-known *painter* and *illustrator*. Father of Boris Pasternak. Left Russia in 1921 and, while retaining his Soviet citizenship, lived first in Germany (Berlin and Munich) and, from 1938, in England. Died in Oxford.

PASTERNAK, Rosa Isidorovna, née Kaufman, 1867–1940. *Pianist.* Her talent was discovered by Anton Rubinstein who sponsored several of her concert tours. Gave up professional career on marriage. Mother of Boris Pasternak.

PETROVSKY, Mikhail Alexeyevich, 1887– . *Critic* and *translator*.

PILNYAK, Boris Andreyevich, pen-name of Vogau, 1894–1937. *Novelist*. First works published in 1915. Novel *The Naked Year* (1922) deals with Civil War and shows life degraded to animal level. *Tale of the Unextinguished Moon* (1926) hints that death on the operating table of War Commissar Frunze (1925) was a "medical murder" ordered by Stalin. *Mahogany* was refused publication in Russia and Pilnyak had it published in Berlin in 1929. This led to his expulsion from the Union of Soviet Writers, a move which signalled the beginning of Stalin's total subjugation of Soviet literature to his own political ends. Pilnyak was arrested in 1937, accused of spying for the Japanese, and either was shot or died in a labour camp.

POLENOV, Vasily Dmitryevich, 1844–1927. *Painter*. Paintings of country life. War artist in Russo-Turkish War of 1877–78. Member of Society for Travelling Art Exhibitions. Painted scenes from the life of Christ (1880's). Elected member of Academy of Art in 1893. After revolution lived in a village now called Polenovo.

PRZYBYSZEWSKI, Stanislaw, 1868–1927. Outstanding Polish *poet* and *playwright*. Wrote plays full of fatalistic terror and poems on the mystical and tragic aspects of love and death, which became very fashionable.

RACHINSKY, Grigory Alexeyevich. One of the moving spirits of the Society of Religious Philosophy. Professor at Moscow University. An advocate of children's religious education.

REBIKOV, Vladimir Ivanovich, 1866–1920. *Composer*. One of the first representatives of modernism in Russian music. A "miniaturist" in music, influenced by impressionism and symbolism, he composed *Fables* based on Krylov and the opera *Christmas Tree* based on Dostoyevsky. Believed in a system of music and mimics which he called "melomimics".

REPIN, Ilya Yefimovich, 1844–1930. Famous *painter*. Studied in Petersburg, Italy and Paris. Active in the Society for travelling Art Exhibitions. Paintings deal with peasant life and historical subjects, e.g. "Ivan the Terrible with his Son" (1885), "The Zaporozhian Cossacks write to the Sultan" (1891). Portraits include those of Tolstoy and other well-known writers and artists and, among foreign celebrities, Eleonora Duse.

RILKE, Rainer Maria, 1875–1926. Regarded as greatest German *poet* since Goethe. Born in Prague. Miserable schooldays at Military School of St Polten 1886–91. Studied in Linz (1892) and at University of Prague (1895–6), before devoting himself to literature. Began serious study of Russian literature at suggestion of Lou

Andréas Salomé. Short visit to Russia, first of many spiritual homes, in 1899; longer visit in 1900. Meeting with Tolstoy. Correspondence and meeting with Leonid Pasternak. 1899–1903: first major work, *The Book of Hours*. 1901: married sculptress, Clara Westhoff. Secretary to Rodin 1902–6. Separated from wife. 1906: completed and published *Book of Images*. 1907–8: publication of *New Poems*. 1909: *Requiem*. 1911–12: wrote first two *Duino Elegies* while staying at the castle of an aristocratic friend at Duino, near Trieste. Lived for short periods in Scandinavia, Italy, Spain and North Africa, always in great distress of spirit. 1922: completed *Duino Elegies* (1923) and the unexpected fifty-five *Sonnets to Orpheus*. Last years spent in Switzerland. Uncollected poems of 1906–26 published posthumously. Died of leukæmia at Valmont, near Montreux.

SADOVSKY, Boris Alexandrovich, b. 1881. Symbolist *poet* and *critic*.

SAPUNOV, Nikolay Nikolayevich, 1880–1912. *Painter*. Studied under Levitan, Korovin, Serov. Visited Italy in 1902. Joined "Blue Rose" group. Painted landscapes: designed scenery for productions of Ibsen's *Hedda Gabler*, Blok's *Balaganchik*, Gozzi's *Turandot*, etc.

SCRIABIN, Alexander Nikolayevich, 1872–1915. *Composer*. Born in Moscow, son of diplomat and pianist. Attended Cadet School. Studied at Moscow Conservatoire (1882–92), winning a Gold Medal as a pianist. 1898–1903: Professor of Piano at Moscow Conservatoire. Early compositions show kinship with Chopin. *Poème Satanique* (1903) echoes Liszt's *Malédiction* and shows Scriabin committing himself to magical view of art. His first symphony (1901) already showed taste for the grandiose; with his fourth piano sonata (1903) he throws off the drawing-room elegance of his early compositions and develops the fragmentation of melody and the ecstatic trills of his maturer period. His idea of music as incantation is explicit in the inscription on the orgiastic fifth piano sonata: "I call you forth to life, hidden influences sunk in the obscure depths of the Creative Spirit, timid germs of life, I bring you boldness!" Scriabin became interested in theosophy and saw himself as the messiah destined to bring about "Final Act", the act of Union between the "Male-Creator and the Female World", by which Spirit was to redeem matter, a great liturgical rite in which all the arts would play their part and which would usher in a new era. Attempted approach to his idea in *Prometheus* "fire poem" for orchestra, piano and *clavier à lumière*; the latter was a first attempt to achieve synthesis of the arts and "counterpoint of the senses": he dreamed of "a musical phrase ending in a scent, a chord resolving itself into colour, a melodic line whose climax is a caress". His most famous composition: *Poème de l'extase*. 1904–10: toured Switzerland, France (where he became acquainted with writings of Madame Blavatsky and Annie Besant), Italy and USA. In 1910 performed in Holland

and in 1914 in Britain. In 1922 his flat in Moscow was made a museum.

SELVINSKY, Ilya Lvovich, 1899–1968. *Poet.* Leader of Constructivists (cf. below). At one time looked like taking Mayakovsky's place. Published first poems in 1926. Of his later works his ballads and songs were the most successful. Wrote poem about Arctic expedition of Chelyuskin in which he had taken part (1933–34). Wrote patriotic verses during 1941–45 war.

(*Constructivists:* a group of young poets organised in 1924. Took over futurists' (cf. note on ASEYEV) interest in technology and other contemporary themes but were less anti-traditional. Believed that a poem should be a "construction" in which, as in engineering, the maximum effect is derived from a given potential. In 1929–30 the group rallied a number of poets to active support of the régime. Broke up in 1930.)

SEROV, Valentin Alexandrovich, 1865–1911. *Painter.* Born in Petersburg, son of composer A. N. Serov and V. S. Serova. Pupil of Repin. Mainly distinguished as portrait painter but also painted scenes of country life and dramatic compositions, e.g. "The Meeting: Arrival of an Exile's Wife". At the end of nineteenth century joined "World of Art" group. During 1905 revolution drew caricatures for the revolutionary press. Protested to Academy of Arts against massacre of 9 January and resigned from Academy when protest was rejected. Portraits include Chaliapin and Stanislavsky. In last years of his life was influenced by contemporary French painting (e.g. his portrait of Ida Rubinstein).

SEVERYANIN, Igor, pen-name of Igor Vasilyevich Lotaryev, 1887–1941. *Poet.* Member of so-called "Ego-Futurists". Facile command of rhythm; vocabulary of modern city life and technology; profuse coining of new words; but had little to express save cheap dreams of luxury and sensuality. Extremely popular after publication of his "Thunder-Seething Cup" (1913). Emigrated; was in Esthonia when it was occupied by the Soviet Union in 1940 and wrote verses greeting the Soviet power.

SHCHEGOLEV, Pavel Yeliseyevich, 1877–1931. *Literary historian.*

SHENROK, Vladimir Ivanovich, 1853–1910. *Literary historian.* Specialised in Gogol.

SHERSHENEVICH, Vadim Gabrielevich, 1893–1942. *Poet.* At first influenced by symbolism, later by futurism, then by imagism (cf. below). Wrote verses which are almost disconnected lists of metaphors. Translator of Shakespeare, Corneille, Baudelaire. Wrote film scenarios, libretti for operettas, etc.

(*Imagism:* A poetic movement organised in 1919 which stressed imagery and metaphor as basis of poetry. Favoured free verse. Introduced coarsest images side by side with the pathetic and the sublime. The imagists in Moscow led a rowdy bohemian life and boasted of their hooliganism. After 1924 the group fell apart.)

SIMONOV, Konstantin Mikhaylovich, 1915–1979. *Poet, novelist, playwright.* Early verse mostly love poetry. Graduated from literary institute of Union of Soviet Writers in 1938. Wrote a patriotic poem about Suvorov in 1939. During Second World War became the most famous lyric poet. Wrote war novels: *Days and Nights, Comrades in Arms,* and plays including the anti-American play *The Russian Question.* After the war mainly active in journalism as editor of *Literaturnaya Gazeta* and *Novy Mir.*

SOLOVYOV, Vladimir Sergeyevich, 1853–1900. *Poet, critic* and most influential Russian nineteenth-century *religious philosopher.*

SOMOV, Konstantin Nikolayevich, 1869–1939. *Painter* and *art critic.* Member of "World of Art" group.

STASOV, Vladimir Vasilyevich, 1824–1906. Art and music *critic.* Keen supporter of the Society for Travelling Art Exhibitions. In 1880's wrote number of books on history of art. Edited published letters of Musorgsky and Glinka.

STEPUN, Fyodor Avgustovich, 1884–19. Stage *producer, writer* and scholar. Author of several novels and of an autobiography which gives an excellent picture of the artistic and literary atmosphere in pre-revolutionary Moscow. Emigrated, lived in Germany.

SUDEYKIN, Sergey Yuryevich, 1883– . *Painter.* Took part in "Blue Rose" and "World of Art" exhibitions. Mainly landscapes, studies for theatre scenery. Exhibited in Paris, 1921.

SURIKOV, Vasily Ivanovich, 1848–1916. *Painter.* Member of Society for Travelling Art Exhibitions. Studied in Petersburg but quarrelled with his conservative professors and moved to Moscow (1877). Vast historical pictures: "The Morning of the Execution of the Streltsy" (1881), "The Boyarina Morozova" (1887), scenes from lives of Stenka Razin, Pugachev, etc.

TABIDZE, Titsian Yustinovich, 1895–1937. Georgian *poet.* Studied at Moscow University. Was one of the founders of the "Blue Horns" group of Georgian symbolist poets (1915). Rallied to Soviet régime after 1921 and helped to found Union of Georgian Writers. At the Congress of Soviet writers in 1934 the Blue Horns group was criticised by the chairman of the Union of Georgian Writers as still being only "fellow-travellers". Tabidze perished in one of the purges in the Thirties.

TIKHONOV, Nikolay Semyonovich, 1896–1979. *Poet.* Fought in First World War and on Red side in Civil War. Wrote war poems 1916–17. Next two books of poems, *The Horde* and *Country Beer* came out in 1922. *The Shadow of a Friend* includes poems written in Poland, Austria, France, Belgium and England, while *Yurga* and *Poems of Kakhetia* are about his experiences in the Caucasus and Central Asia.

He was attracted by strong personalities, grandiose scenery and dangerous undertakings. His experiences in beleaguered Leningrad are described in his war poems, *The Fiery Year*.

TIKHONOV, A. N. Editor of *Russky Sovremennik*, a periodical in which Pasternak published works in poetry and prose in the Twenties.

TOLSTOY, Alexey Konstantinovich, 1817–75. *Poet* and *dramatist*. The Moscow Art Theatre opened its first season (October 1898) with his play, *Tsar Fyodor Ivanovich*.

TOLSTOY, Andrey Lvovich, 1877–1916. Leo Tolstoy's third son.

TOLSTOY, Ilya Lvovich, 1866–1933. Author of *Reminiscences of my Father*. Leo Tolstoy's second son.

TOLSTOY, Sergey Lvovich, 1863–1947. Leo Tolstoy's eldest son, author of monograph, *My Father in the Seventies*.

TRETYAKOV, Sergey Mikhailovich, 1892–1947. *Playwright*. Author of *Roar, China!* produced by Meyerhold. Disappeared during purges of 1937–38.

TRUBETSKOY, Prince Nikolay Sergeyevich, 1890–1938. Great linguist and founder of a new phonological theory. Emigrated in 1920 and became professor of comparative philology at the University of Vienna, a post which he held from 1923 until his death.

TRUBETSKOY, Prince Pavel (Paolo) Petrovich, 1867–1938. *Sculptor*. Born and died in Italy. Worked in France and USA. Except for brief visits between 1907 and 1914, lived in Russia only from 1897–1906, and hardly knew Russian. A brilliant sculptor of impressionist tendencies, he excelled in equestrian subjects. Works include "Tolstoy on Horseback" (1899) and equestrian monument to Alexander III unveiled in Petersburg in 1909.

TRUBETSKOY, Prince Sergey Nikolayevich, 1862–1905. Leading *philosopher*. Took active part in liberal opposition in 1904–05. Died soon after being elected Rector of Moscow University.

TRUBETSKOY, Prince Yevgeny Nikolayevich, 1863–1920. Brother of Sergey. Taught theory of law at Moscow University. As political writer fought a hopeless battle against the two "apocalyptic beasts of reaction and revolution."

TSVETAYEVA, Marina Ivanovna, 1892–1941. *Poet*. Began literary work in 1910. Left Russia in 1922 to join her husband Yefron who, after fighting as White officer in Civil War, was evacuated with remnants of Wrangel's army to Constantinople and later found his way to Prague. The family (there were a son and daughter) lived in reduced circumstances in Prague, then in Paris. In 1939 they decided to return to Russia (Yefron after fighting on Republican side in the Spanish Civil War). On their return Yefron was arrested and perished; the daughter was also arrested; the son was killed at the front early in the war. Tsvetayeva herself was banished to a provincial town, Yelabuga, where she could not work – even as a charwoman – and hanged herself on 31 August 1941.

TVARDOVSKY, Alexander Trifonovich, 1910–71. *Poet.* First poems appeared in 1930. Achieved fame with three long narrative poems, "The Land of Muravia", "Vasily Tvorkin" and "The House by the Roadside". Highly imaginative realism.

TYUTCHEV, Fyodor Ivanovich, 1803–73. Lyric *poet.* Served in Diplomatic Service (1822–39) and in Censorship Department (1844–73). Wrote about three hundred short poems. Striking use of colloquialism against background of conventional poetic vocabulary of the beginning of the century. Certain lines from Tyutchev's nature poetry read like anticipations of Pasternak.

ULYANOV, Nikolay Pavlovich, 1875–1949. *Painter.* Studied under Serov. Portraits include those of Chekhov and Stanislavsky. Did much theatre work including settings for *Les fourberies de Scapin, Carmen,* etc. His memoirs were published posthumously in 1952.

VASNETSOV, Appollinary Mikhailovich, 1856–1933. *Painter.* Born in Northern Russia, son of a village priest. Joined Society for Travelling Art Exhibitions and became well known as landscape painter, especially of Urals and Siberian scenes. From 1890 lived in Moscow and painted pictures of its historic past. Elected to Academy in 1900. Designed scenery for operas *Khovanshchina, Sadko,* etc. Attacked impressionism.

VASNETSOV, Victor Mikhailovich, 1848–1926. *Painter.* Elder brother of Appollinary. Associated with Repin and V. V. Stasov. In 1878 moved to Moscow. Painted subjects from Russian folk-lore and medieval history, e.g. "Ivan the Terrible" and "Bogatyri" (often reproduced).

VERHAEREN, Emile. 1855–1916. Belgian modernist *poet.*

VRUBEL, Mikhail Alexandrovich, 1856–1910. *Painter.* Member of Academy from 1905 on. Well known as book illustrator, icon-painter, portrait-painter, muralist and theatrical designer.

YASHVILI, Paolo Dzhibraelovich, 1895–1937. Georgian *poet.* Went to Paris on eve of First World War. On his return in 1916 became a leader of the "Blue Horns" group (cf. note on TABIDZE). During Menshevik occupation in Georgia (1918–21) his poetry reflected ardent Georgian nationalism. But he is said to have welcomed the establishment of Soviet rule and wrote a poem on Lenin's death and in praise of socialist system. Translated Pushkin, Lermontov and Mayakovsky into Georgian. Committed suicide.

YESENIN, Sergey Alexandrovich. 1895–1925. Great lyric *poet.* Born in Central Russia, son of a peasant. Went to parish school, then studied at a free University in Moscow while working as printer's reader. Went to Petrograd, met Blok there and decided to stay. Welcomed revolution, especially for what he hoped it would do for peasants, but was disillusioned by Bolshevik proletarisation and industrialisation of country life. Joined imagists in 1919 (cf. note on SHERSHENEVICH) and took part in their rowdy café life. Married Isadora Duncan in 1922 and went abroad with her; they separated a year later and he returned to Russia. Suffered a mental breakdown and in December 1925 cut his wrists, wrote a farewell poem in his own blood and hanged himself. Particularly memorable for his earliest and latest poems evoking Russian countryside. Enjoyed enormous popularity in his lifetime, particularly with the younger generation.

ZABOLOTSKY, Nikolay, 1903–58. *Poet* and *translator*. He was close to the futurists and belonged to the "Oberiuts" in the late Twenties. Early poems were increasingly grotesque parodies, sounding like nonsense verse but with a satirical edge critical of the new régime. Disappeared for several years and re-emerged in the Fifties, writing in more orthodox style. Works include translation in verse of twelfth-century epic, *The Lay of Prince Igor's Campaigns*.

p. 16
p. 17 chopin
p. 18 Scriabin

Notes on *Poems 1955–1959*

The Russian text of these poems first appeared in the Soviet periodical *Znamya*: "I want the heart of the matter", "Fame's not a pretty sight", EVE, NO TITLE, CHANGE, SPRING IN THE FOREST, JULY, PICKING MUSHROOMS, FIRST SNOW. BREAD was first printed in another periodical, *Oktyabr*.

The first thirty-four poems (those written in 1955 and 1956) also appeared in Russia in the Italian edition of *An Essay in Autobiography* (Feltrinelli, Milan, 1959), and in France and Germany.

1. The Russian word is "stand", as the congregation stands through a Russian Orthodox service.
2. This is a Russian recipe for making glue out of cherries.
3. Adam Mickiewicz (pronounced Mitskyevich, with the accent on the second syllable), 1798–1855. Polish romantic poet, who championed the revolutionary movement in his own country, in Western Europe, and in Russia where he spent five years (1824–29). He was associated with the Decembrist movement and was a friend of Pushkin.
4. Alexander Blok (1880–1921). Russian poet. A symbolist. He greeted the revolution of 1917 as a cleansing storm. *The Twelve* (cf. p. 119) is an apocalyptic vision of the revolution, personified by twelve Red Army men led by Christ. 'Book Three' (cf. p. 119) is the third volume of Blok's collected works.
5. Church in Moscow dedicated to Saints Boris and Gleb, who were martyred in Illyria in the second century (because they erected a cross on a heathen temple which they were ordered to build).
6. Zim, Ziss: Soviet cars. Tatra: Czech car.
7. Pasternak translated Schiller's *Mary Stuart*. The play was very successful on the Russian stage.
8. Tsar Gorokh (literally Tsar Pea): Russian folk-tale figure. "In the time of Tsar Gorokh" is the equivalent of "once upon a time".